# The Annual Diagram

## Forecasting Using
## the 45° Graphic Ephermeris

Reinhold Ebertin

Translated by Linda Kratzsch

ISBN-10: 0-86690-605-3
ISBN-13: 978-0-86690-605-0

Translator: Linda Kratzsch
Cover Design: Jack Cipolla

Published by:
American Federation of Astrologers, Inc.
6535 S. Rural Road
Tempe AZ 85283

www.astrologers.com

Printed in the United States of America

# Contents

# Preface

The word "transit" means a "crossing over," or the passage of the stellar bodies in motion over the sensitive points of the cosmogram (or horoscope)—the stellar bodies, the points of Midheaven and Ascendant, and their aspects. In practice this means taking up the natal chart and the ephemeris containing the daily stellar positions and checking these day by day to see which transiting stellar bodies are crossing over the individual points in the cosmogram.

The symbol we use for the transiting bodies is "t"; an "r" is the designation for the positions as marked in the natal chart. According to custom, the natal chart, from which all calculations are derived, was known as the radix (root) horoscope or simply radix, and its designation.

Therefore, when we say Jupiter t = Sun r, we mean that Jupiter is currently missing the natal Sun. We avoid the terms astrology and horoscope because today they are generally misunderstood and misinterpreted. The misuse of these concepts is extant in the daily press with its solar astrology and weekly horoscopes. For this reason we speak of cosmobiology, meaning the correlation between the cosmic processes and living creatures, as well as earthly events. However, we do not maintain that the stellar bodies alone exercise an influence. Rather, heredity, environment, parental home, vocation, the times in which he lives, etc. also have a decisive effect on the individual.

As we have learned from recent research, which was purely cosmobiological and not astrological, the electromagnetic fields in the solar universe have to be considered as the transmitters of information. This information is altered by the direct influence of the stellar bodies, and these changes in turn influence brain activity, the stimulation of the nerve cells, the heartbeat, etc.

The term cosmogram designates any sort of record made of the stellar configurations, not only of births but also of events. The term horoscope is generally taken to mean only the natal chart, and often not even that. For the daily press, the solar position alone is the same as horoscope, without consideration of the other stellar bodies.

By transit, therefore, we mean a crossing point which arises when a planet in motion passes over a particular point in the cosmogram.

The graphic 45° ephemeris gives us a quick and easy, readable picture of an entire year and enables us to ascertain when positive or negative reaction points make their appearance, corresponding to either good or bad periods in life, to health or illness, to success or failure, or to harmony or disharmony.

*Reinhold Ebertin*

Chapter 1

# The 45-degree System

The 90° circle was introduced in Germany many years ago. When using it, the signs Aries, Cancer, Libra, and Capricorn are located from 0° to 30°; the signs Taurus, Leo, Scorpio, Aquarius from 30° to 60°; and the signs Gemini, Virgo, Sagittarius, and Pisces are from 60° to 90°. The advantage of this is that in this system all the stellar bodies forming a conjunction, square, and opposition are located in the same place, and opposite them are the bodies in semisquare and sesquiquadrate. Therefore, it is not necessary to look up all the aspects in the cosmogram, but rather only those points showing an aspect divisible by 90°. All of these aspects are thus found together.

This system does not contain the sextiles (60°) or the trines (120°). Traditional astrology often considers the sextiles and trines as favorable and the other aspects as unfavorable. This has proved to be false. Years ago I pointed out the fact that the sextile and trine are aspects that correspond to a condition or state, while the conjunction, square, and opposition indicate a certain degree of tension or potential, and when they appear as transits, something happens, a situation is triggered. There is substantiation for the predominance of such "aspects of potential" in the cosmograms of prominent or successful individuals, whereas the sextiles and trines are more in evidence in the cosmograms of everyday persons, of those who do not stand out in the crowd. It has also been

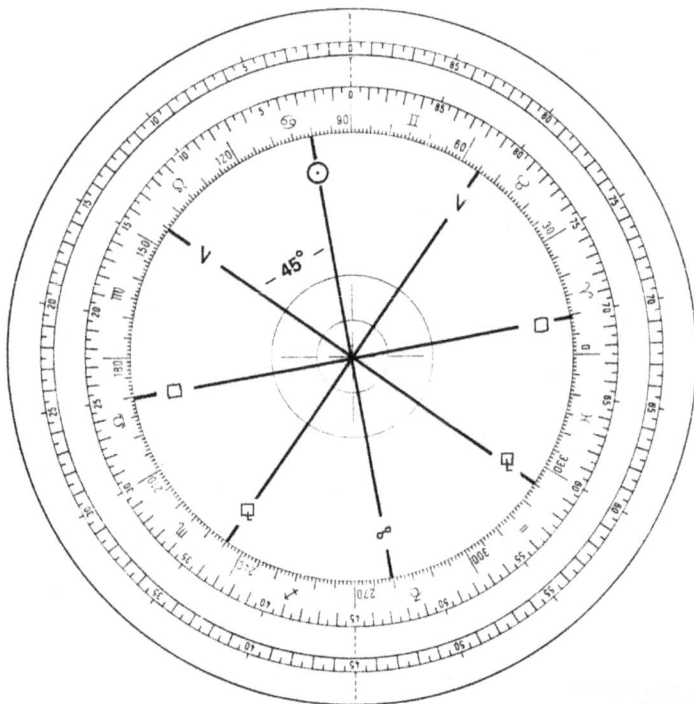

*Figure 1*

found that recognition, advancement, and success are signaled by aspects of 45° (semisquare) and 135° (sesquiquadrate).

Figure 1 shows the aspects of potential. For example, when the Sun is at 10 Cancer, the aspect points, or reaction points, are found at 25 Leo (45°), 10 Libra (90°), 25 Scorpio (135°), 10 Aries (90°) or 25 Taurus (45°). Therefore, if a transiting planet is located at these points, it enters into relationship with the natal Sun and the result is a reaction, the character of which is determined by the nature of the triggering body.

The aspects named are derived from the progressive division of the circle (into halves, quarters, and eighths). This same system is

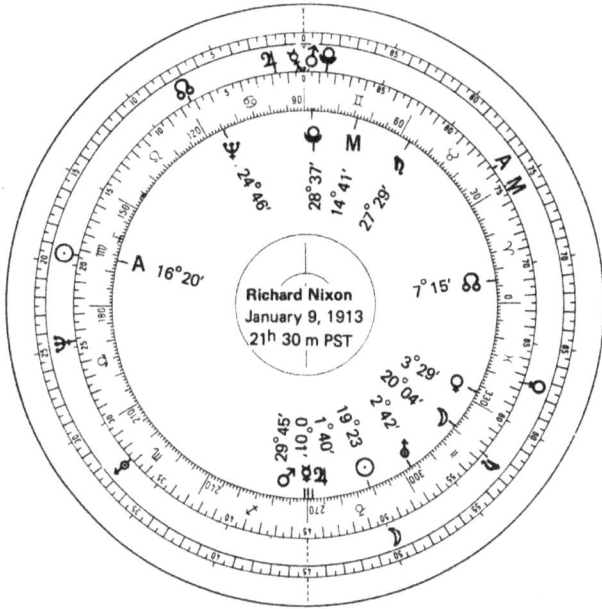

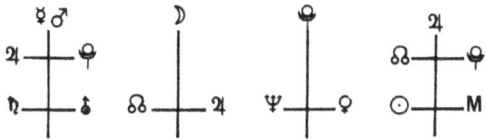

**Figure 2**

used for the meteorological wind rose, a diagrammatical representation of the winds and directions. The number eight has since prehistoric times been considered as a symbol for regularity and symmetry.

I developed the combined chart form, which contains the customary zodiacal circle with the twelve signs and the division into degrees, but surrounding this is the 90° circle. On looking at the cosmogram of former president Richard Nixon (see Figure 2), the Sun is in the inner circle at 19 Capricorn, and has to be transcribed to the first third of the 90° circle. The positions of the individual

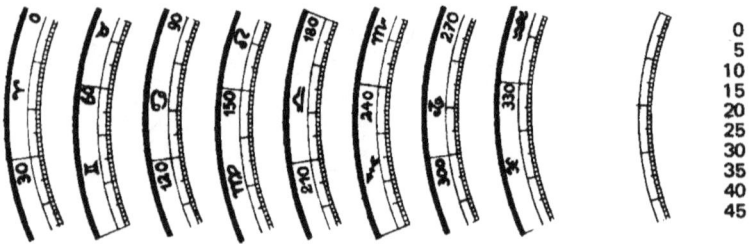

*Figure 3*

bodies in Aries (Moon's Node) and Cancer (Neptune) along with
the planets in Capricorn also have to be transcribed to the first
third. In contrast, however, the Moon is located at 20 Aquarius and
must be placed at 20° of the second third or at 50° in the outer circle. This is also true for Saturn, located at 27 Taurus. The planets
in the mutable signs (Gemini, Virgo, Sagittarius, and Pisces) are
placed in the last sector. Venus at 3 Pisces is placed at 63. In the
45° system, those points also coincide which oppose one another
in the 90° circle. The following figures illustrate the system in
more detail. In the beginning, this system may seem somewhat
difficult, but with practice, the merits of the system will be
recognized.

Figure 3 shows the eight sectors of the zodiac in one row, and
the last sector shows the division into 45°. If, for example, there are
planets at 0 Aries, Cancer, Libra, or Capricorn, or at 15 Taurus,
Leo, Scorpio, or Aquarius, these will also be in the same position
in the 45° system.

Figure 4 shows the same scheme. The various factors according
to Nixon's natal chart have been entered in the separate sections
and summarized in the last column.

| 360° Circle | | | | | | | | 45° Scale |
|---|---|---|---|---|---|---|---|---|
| 00° ♈ | 15° ♉ | 0° ♋ | 15° ♌ | 0° ♎ | 15° ♏ | 0° ♑ ☿ | 15° ♒ | 0° |
| 01 | 16 | 01 | 16 | 01 | 16 | 01 ♃ | 16 | 01 ☿ |
| 02 | 17 | 02 | 17 | 02 | 17 | 02 | 17 | 02 ♃ |
| 03 | 18 | 03 | 18 | 03 | 18 | 03 | 18 | 03 |
| 04 | 19 | 04 | 19 | 04 | 19 | 04 | 19 | 04 |
| 05 | 20 | 05 | 20 | 05 | 20 | 05 | 20 ☽ | 05 ☽ |
| 06 | 21 | 06 | 21 | 06 | 21 | 06 | 21 | 06 |
| 07 ♌ | 22 | 07 | 22 | 07 | 22 | 07 | 22 | 07 ☋ |
| 08 | 23 | 08 | 23 | 08 | 23 | 08 | 23 | 08 |
| 09 | 24 | 09 | 24 | 09 | 24 | 09 | 24 | 09 |
| 10 | 25 | 10 | 25 | 10 | 25 | 10 | 25 | 10 |
| 11 | 26 | 11 | 26 | 11 | 26 | 11 | 26 | 11 |
| 12 | 27 ♄ | 12 | 27 | 12 | 27 | 12 | 27 | 12 ♄ |
| 13 | 28 | 13 | 28 | 13 | 28 | 13 | 28 | 13 |
| 14 | 29 | 14 | 29 | 14 | 29 | 14 | 29 | 14 |
| 15 | 00 ♊ | 15 | 00 ♍ | 15 | 00 ♐ | 15 | 00 ♓ | 15 |
| 16 | 01 | 16 | 01 | 16 | 01 | 16 | 01 | 16 |
| 17 | 02 | 17 | 02 | 17 | 02 | 17 | 02 | 17 |
| 18 | 03 | 18 | 03 | 18 | 03 | 18 | 03 | 18 |
| 19 | 04 | 19 | 04 | 19 | 04 | 19 | 04 | 19 ♀ |
| 20 | 05 | 20 | 05 | 20 | 05 | 20 ☉ | 05 | 20 ☉ |
| 21 | 06 | 21 | 06 | 21 | 06 | 21 | 06 | 21 |
| 22 | 07 | 22 | 07 | 22 | 07 | 22 | 07 | 22 |
| 23 | 08 | 23 | 08 | 23 | 08 | 23 | 08 | 23 |
| 24 | 09 | 24 | 09 | 24 | 09 | 24 | 09 | 24 |
| 25 | 10 | 25 ♆ | 10 | 25 | 10 | 25 | 10 | 25 ♆ |
| 26 | 11 | 26 | 11 | 26 | 11 | 26 | 11 | 26 |
| 27 | 12 | 27 | 12 | 27 | 12 | 27 | 12 | 27 |
| 28 | 13 | 28 | 13 | 28 | 13 | 28 | 13 | 28 |
| 29 | 14 | 29 | 14 | 29 | 14 | 29 | 14 | 29 |
| 00 ♉ | 15 M | 06 ♌ | 15 | 00 ♏ | 15 | 00 - | 15 | 30 M |
| 01 | 16 | 01 | 16 A | 01 | 16 | 01 | 16 | 31 A |
| 02 | 17 | 02 | 17 | 02 | 17 | 02 | 17 | 32 |
| 03 | 18 | 03 | 18 | 03 | 18 | 03 | 18 | 33 |
| 04 | 19 | 04 | 19 | 04 | 19 | 04 | 19 | 34 |
| 05 | 20 | 05 | 20 | 05 | 20 | 05 | 20 | 35 |
| 06 | 21 | 06 | 21 | 06 | 21 | 06 | 21 | 36 |
| 07 | 22 | 07 | 22 | 07 | 22 | 07 | 22 | 37 |
| 08 | 23 | 08 | 23 | 08 | 23 | 08 | 23 | 38 |
| 09 | 24 | 09 | 24 | 09 | 24 | 09 | 24 | 39 |
| 10 | 25 | 10 | 25 | 10 | 25 | 10 | 25 | 40 |
| 11 | 26 | 11 | 26 | 11 | 26 | 11 | 26 | 41 |
| 12 | 27 | 12 | 27 | 12 | 27 | 12 | 27 | 42 |
| 13 | 28 | 13 | 28 | 13 | 28 | 13 | 28 | 43 |
| 14 | 29 ♀ | 14 | 29 | 14 | 29 | 14 | 29 | 44 ♀ |
| 15 | 00 ♋ | 15 | 00 ♎ | 15 | 00 ♑ ♂ | 15 | 00 ♈ | 45 ♂ |

## Chapter 2

# Graphic 45-degree Ephemeris

An excerpt from the graphic 45° ephemeris for 1970 is shown in Figure 5. It has time and space as its components. The time can be read from the top of the page, where we find the division of the year into months and days. A vertical line running to the bottom of the page is drawn for every tenth day.

On the right and left sides, the graduated scales indicate the sectors of the zodiac. Three columns are given on the left side to facilitate making entries. In the case of a planet located in Aries, Cancer, Libra, or Capricorn, one would be concerned with the first column. For a planet in Taurus, Leo, Scorpio, or Aquarius, the second column is applicable. A planet occupying Gemini, Virgo, Sagittarius, or Pisces will be entered in the third column. On the right side is the scale of degrees running from 0 to 45. This scale also serves as a guideline for the ruler when drawing the lines extending from one side to another.

The stellar orbits for the year in question in the 45° system are entered in the inside space. In order to make a simultaneous record of the relevant signs, these are likewise entered. At the beginning of the year, Uranus is at 9 Libra, Neptune is at 0 Sagittarius, Saturn at 2 Taurus, and Jupiter is at 0 Scorpio. The Jupiter-Saturn opposition was exact in December 1969, when there was an influenza epidemic, which is very typical of this opposition.

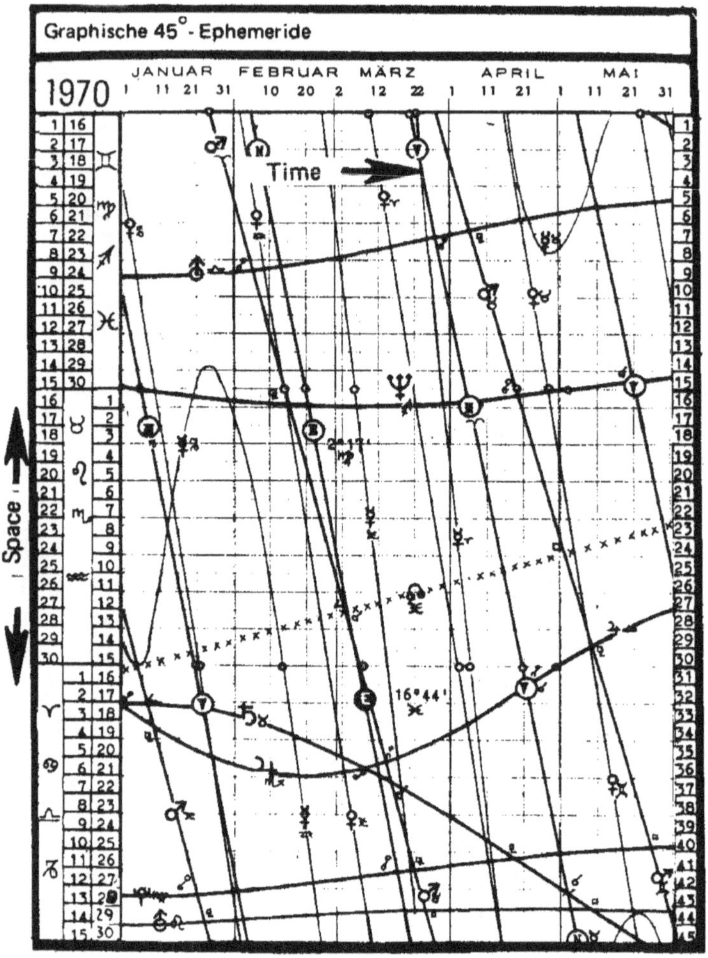

*Figure 5*

Along the solar orbit we see several small circles. When such a circle contains an N, this means New Moon; accordingly, F stands for Full Moon (V is used in German charts). An E designates an eclipse, either an E in a white circle, meaning a lunar eclipse, or an E in a black circle, standing for a solar eclipse. The number of degrees given alongside indicates the degree of the solar eclipse.

The advantage of the graphic ephemeris is that it is in fact a pictorial representation, encompassing all configurations due. Far below, on January 21, we find that Mars forms an opposition to Pluto. At the same time, the Sun at Full Moon is square to Saturn. For this reason, a cold-wave (Sun = Saturn) and natural disasters could be expected at that time. There was a slight earthquake in southern Germany and also a volcanic eruption on the island of New Britain. With the aid of the graphic ephemeris observations can be made of the many various events on Earth and of natural phenomena.

When the orbits are slanted downward, this means the stellar body is moving directly. In the case of an orbit curving toward the top, the body is apparently retrogressive as seen from the earth. The more slanted the orbit, the faster the body is moving; the more the orbit approaches the horizontal plane, the slower the motion of the stellar body.

Chapter 3

# Practical Application
# of the 45-degree Ephemeris

Several examples will demonstrate how to make practical application of the graphic ephemeris. Let us first take some examples from the realm of politics where prognostication has proven true.

**Nixon's Election Configuration**

Figure 6 is the result of the transcription of the positions in the 45° scheme according to the table given in Figure 4. The various crossing points have been marked, the small circles indicating positive configurations and the black dots negative ones. At that time Richard Nixon and Hubert Humphrey were opponents in the presidential race. It seemed that Humphrey would win since he had the better configurations throughout the year (Figure 7). Nixon was especially hampered by aspects of Saturn, which transited the position lines of Moon's Node, Saturn, Venus, Sun, in succession, and then maintains for months the square to Neptune. The short-term Jupiter transits over Venus and Sun in July and over MC, AS, and Uranus in September are poor compensation. But then came a turnaround. At the end of September, Uranus transited Mercury, which it did again at the end of October just before the election of November 5, 1968. In the bottom part of the ephemeris we find Jupiter transiting Pluto and Mars at the beginning of November. Finally, there were transits of Sun and Mars over Mercury

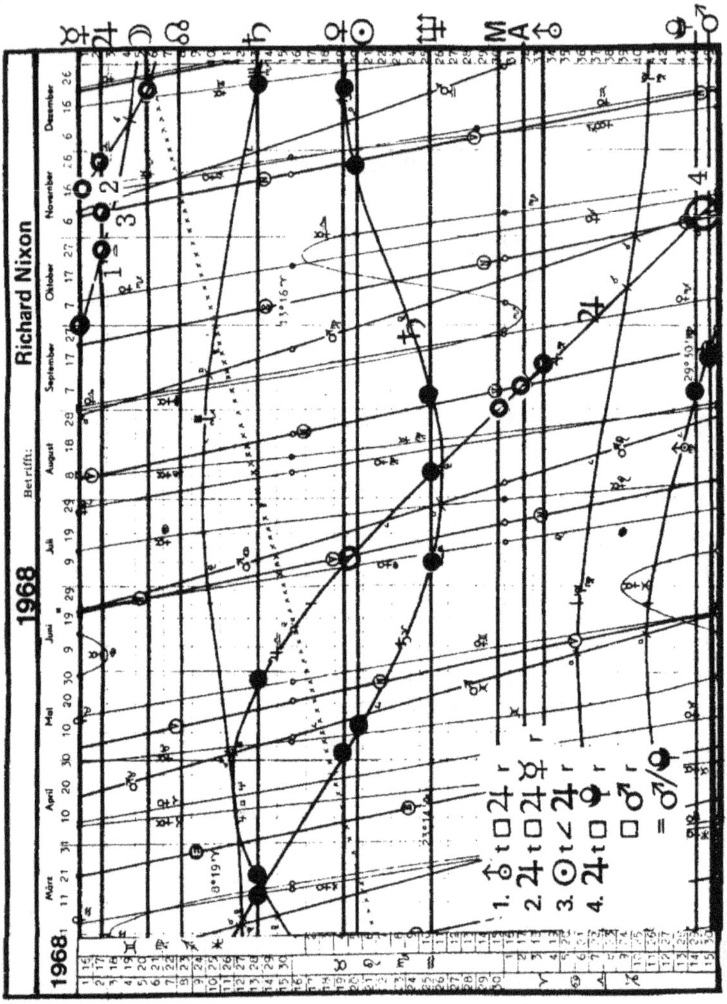

*Figure 6*

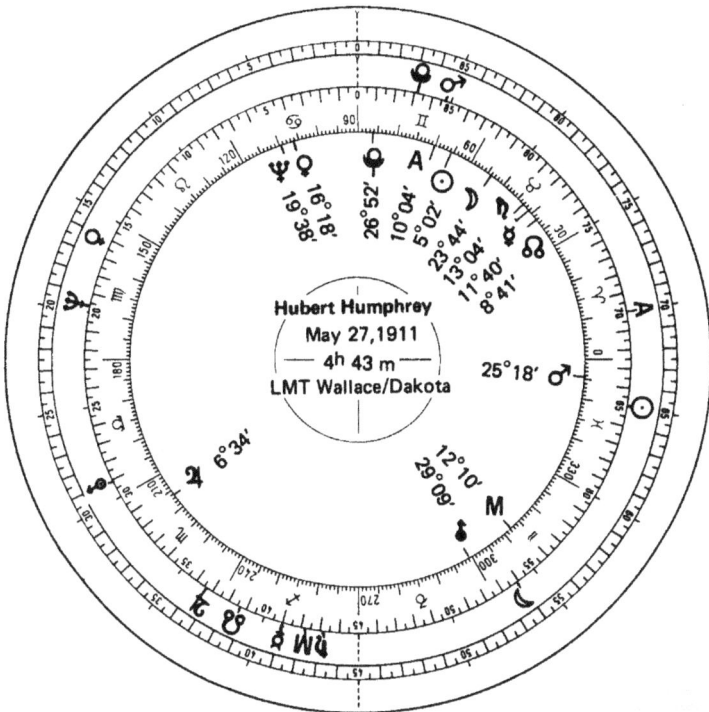

*Figure 7*

and Jupiter (at the very top). Altogether, this is quite an accumulation of positive aspects at the time of the election. It was only in December that negative aspects became effective in the form of transiting Neptune over Saturn, and transiting Saturn over the Sun.

Humphrey's annual diagram (Figure 8) shows that as late as October he still had a number of good Jupiter transits. However, as the day of election approached (November 5), Jupiter, Mars, and the Sun were clustered on the position line of Saturn below, and Saturn itself transited the Sun and Neptune. This synastry allowed me to prognosticate Nixon's victory, and this was possible half a year before the election.

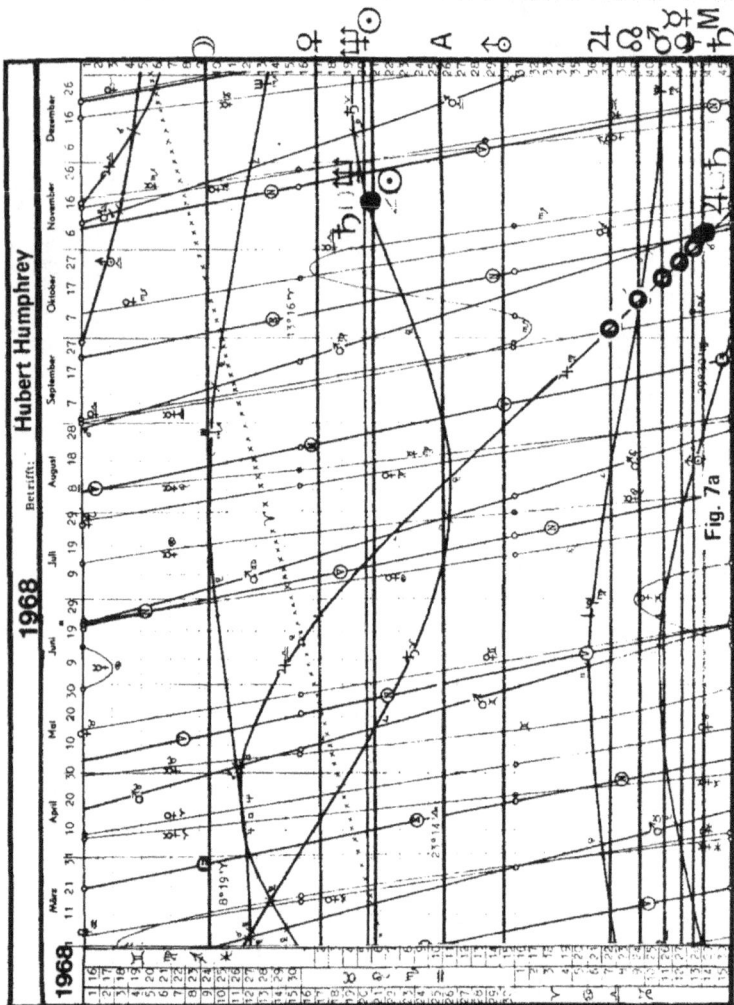

*Figure 8*

# Chapter 4

# Graphic Ephemeris
# and Structural Picture

Of prime concern in the graphic 45° ephemeris are not only the transits or the reaction points but also the cosmic condition can be attached to the transiting body or what role it plays in the structural picture. These are important factors to be taken into account when formulating the interpretation.

In the case of Nixon's cosmogram (Figure 2), we can see that Mercury and Mars are located at the midpoint of Jupiter/Pluto. In addition, Mercury and Mars are found at Saturn/Uranus. This is in fact the really decisive success configuration in Nixon's cosmogram, since according to *The Combination of Stellar Influences*:

Jupiter/Pluto indicates striving for power.

Mercury = Jupiter/Pluto: talent for speaking, desire to influence the masses, advertising campaign (election campaign).

Mars = Jupiter/Pluto: organizational talent, ability to enthuse others, desire to achieve great things.

This natal configuration was transited by Jupiter and Uranus, and means:

Uranus = Jupiter/Pluto: fanatical plans for reform and innovation, quick exploitation of any situation, sudden reform, rapid development, change and transformation.

Jupiter = Jupiter/Pluto: successful outcome of a striving for power, i.e., the succession to a position of power and leadership.

One important thing to remember with the graphic ephemeris is that it does not simply end at the bottom of the page with 45°. Rather, when an orbit hits the bottom, it recommences at the top. This ephemeris must be imagined as a kind of roll on which 0° and 45° complement one another.

The conclusion to be drawn from this discussion is that the transits cannot be evaluated for themselves, and that it is also necessary to investigate which position the transited factors take up in the natal chart.

Only the most important midpoints were mentioned above regarding Nixon's cosmogram. Mercury and Mars are also located at Saturn/Uranus and therefore severe nervous strain and decisions under pressure are indicated. However, Jupiter's arrival at this midpoint indicates according to *The Combination of Stellar Influences*: happy release of tensions. This is perfectly applicable in this case in that the month-long tension before the election finds its fortunate release in the victory.

### Martin Luther King, Jr. and Robert Kennedy

Both of these cases occurred under similar Mars-Pluto aspects.

In an article published at the end of March 1968, I pointed out the "catastrophe configuration of April 6, 1968." My words were: "Due to MA-135-PL, brute force, accidents, murders are involved. . . ." Those persons whose cosmograms contain correlations between this configuration and the individual planetary positions are most particularly endangered.

The assassination of Martin Luther King, Jr. occurred April 4, 1968, at 6:01 p.m. local time in Memphis, Tennessee. Since this city is located 90° west of Greenwich, meaning a time difference

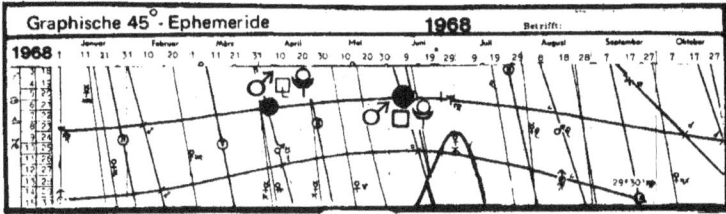

*Figure 9*

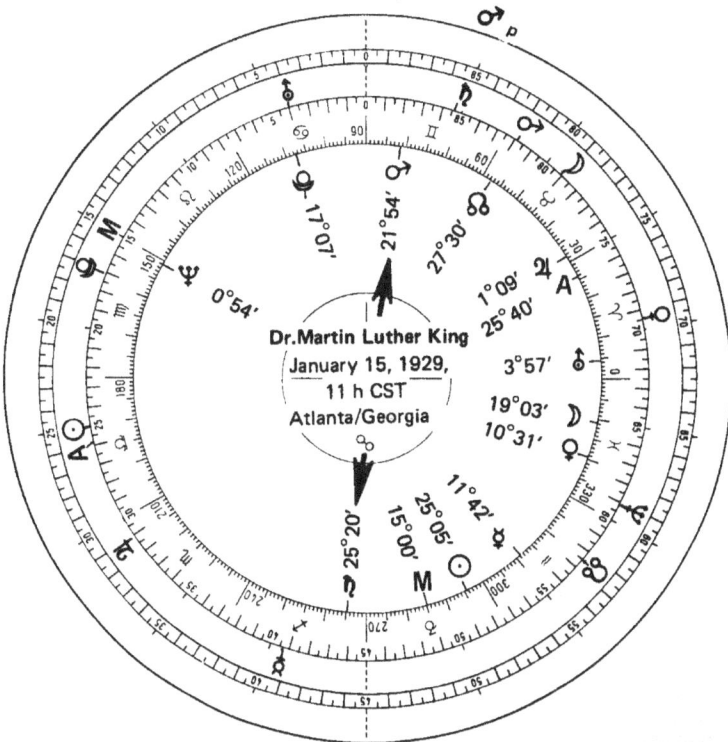

*Figure 10*

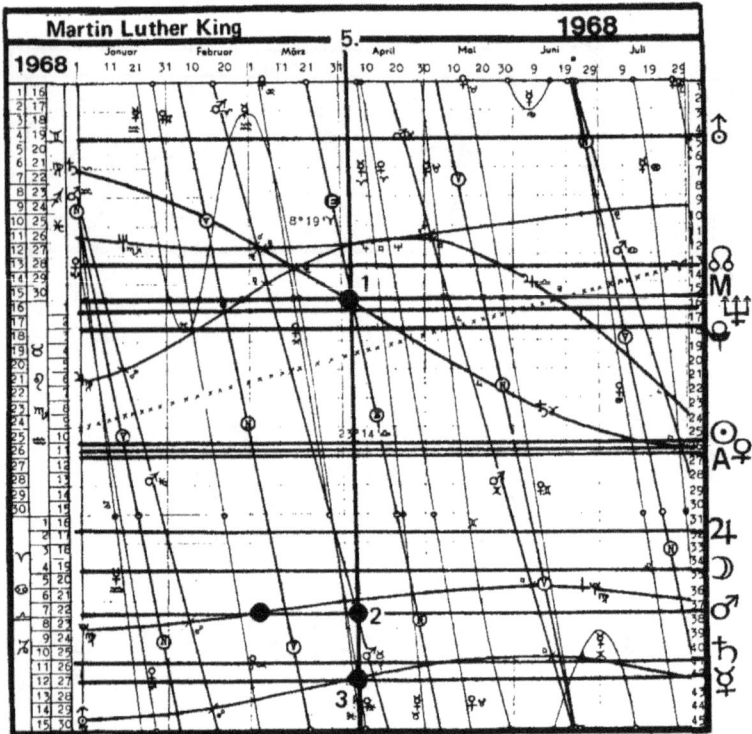

*Figure 11*

of six hours, we can read of the midnight position (0h) on April 5 from the ephemeris. We then find in the 90° circle the MC of the catastrophe configuration directly on the axis Mars-Pluto. This configuration in turn coincides with the King's MC in his cosmogram at the midpoint Sun/Uranus.

Very striking to the eye in King's cosmogram (Figure 9) is the opposition of Mars to Saturn. Both factors can be found in the upper right in the 90° circle. (Adolf Hitler had a similar constellation at the time of his demise, when Mars in progression reached the square to Saturn.) Mars-Saturn is a well-known death configuration. Progressed Mars is at 25 Gemini in an exact opposition to Saturn. It must be emphasized time and again that significant

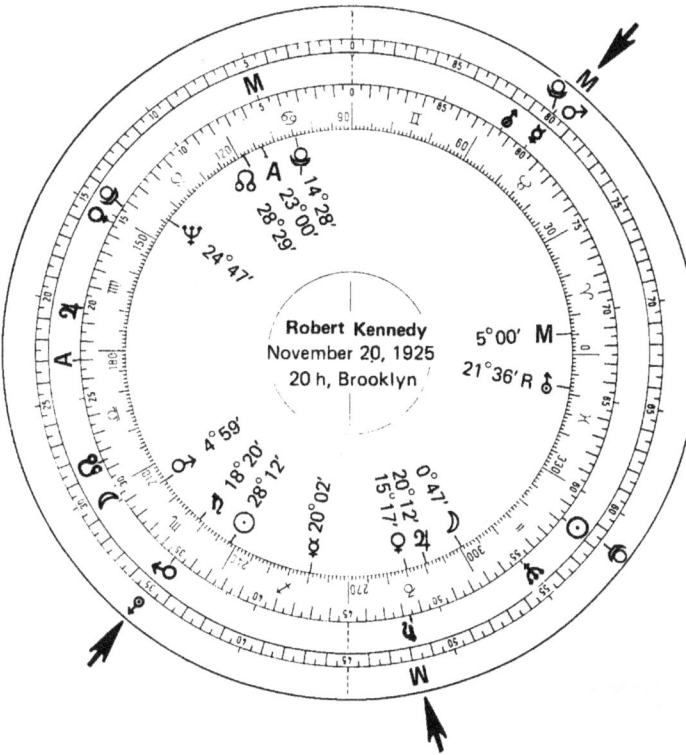

**Figure 12**

events in life may be determined by the directions, but they are triggered by the corresponding transits.

One other decisive configuration contained in the cosmogram is that of Pluto at the Midheaven opposition Neptune at Sun/Uranus and Uranus/AS. In this context Pluto = MC means that the native can attain recognition and power and that he sees in his position a kind of mission in life. The Neptune opposition can undermine this position and lead to great disappointments. *The Combination of Stellar Influences* gives us the following statements on these positions at Sun/Uranus and Uranus/AS: radical reformer (as a black leader), tragic experiences, sudden events and severe

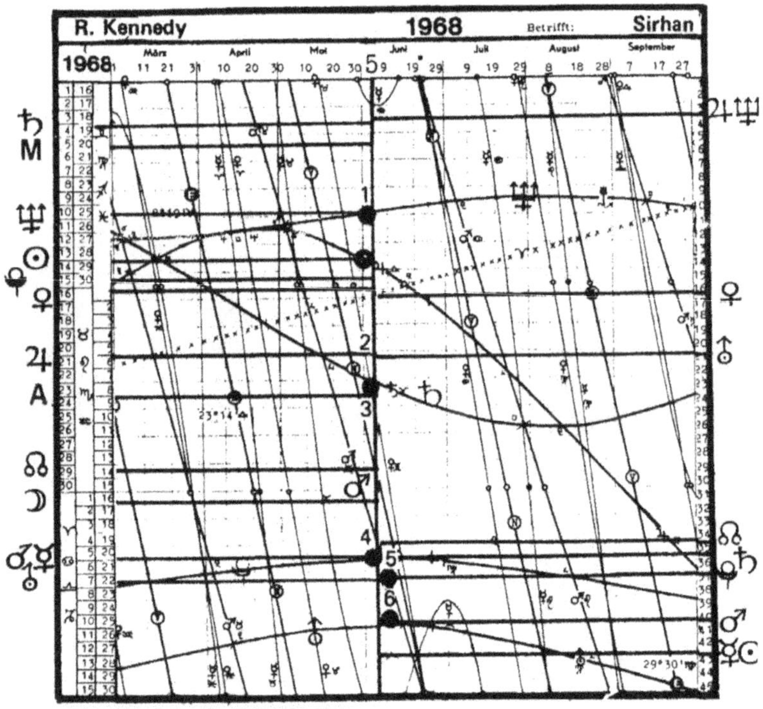

*Figure 13*

shock, desire to overcome poor conditions and difficult situations, excitement and upset. This configuration was triggered by Saturn pointing to sudden hindrances, separations, upsets.

Let us now take a look at the graphic ephemeris in Figure 11. Here we see transiting Saturn at the time of the assassination to be over the Midheaven and Saturn (1), triggered by the Sun. At (2), Pluto had already transited Mars (use of force, murder).

However, this configuration was not triggered by Mars until April 5. At (3), Mercury and Uranus transit Saturn and Mercury respectively (separation). If, therefore, the annual diagram had been consulted beforehand, a warning would have been possible.

Around June 5, 1968, Mars again transited Pluto, this time in

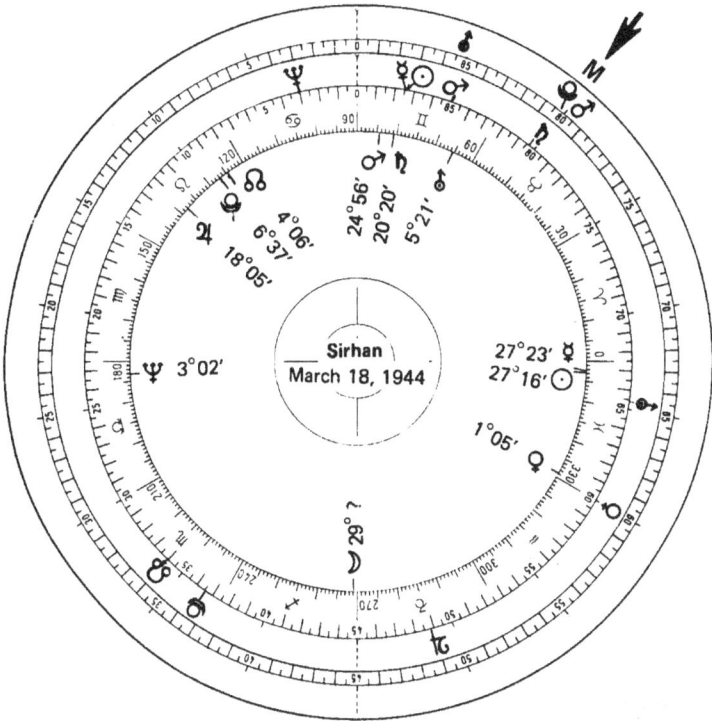

*Figure 14*

opposition. On this day, Robert Kennedy was murdered by Sirhan Sirhan. In May 1968, I had written in an article: "MA-90-PL, initiating another period of catastrophes and acts of violence." At the moment of the crime, the transiting Midheaven entered this configuration.

Critical directions are evident in Kennedy's cosmogram (Figure 12). The Midheaven entered an opposition to Saturn, Uranus was opposition Uranus, and Pluto was square Sun.

Consulting the graphic ephemeris for June 1968 (Figure 13), we find at (1) transiting Neptune aspecting natal Neptune by semisquare, which is detrimental in that the natal chart has Neptune = Sun/Saturn (with an orb of 1.5°), meaning a physical crisis. At (2), Jupiter transits the Sun, which in fact should be favorable. Shortly before, Kennedy received great applause at a meeting. But Sun at Mars/Uranus in the radix can also indicate the danger of injury and mishap. At (3), Saturn crosses over the Ascendant, pointing to separation. A similar configuration as in the case of Martin Luther King, Jr. can be found at (4), where Pluto transiting Mars was triggered by transiting Mars.

It is also interesting to look at the cosmogram of the murderer, Sirhan Sirhan (Figure 14). In this case, however, the birth time is unavailable. Even so, many configurations can be read using the graphic ephemeris and without the Midheaven and Ascendant.

At the same place where Kennedy's Mercury and Mars are located, we see Saturn and Pluto, triggered by transiting Pluto and Mars (5). The use of force can also be read from Uranus transiting Mars (6).

### DeGaulle in the Face of Defeat

General Charles DeGaulle, who always called himself the liberator of France, was fully convinced that only he could properly guide the people and bring them good. In the final years, however, unrest and discontent increased. In the natal chart the positive and negative configurations are in constant equilibrium. Let us observe Pluto and its aspects. Many persons of DeGaulle's own age have the conjunction with Neptune, and there is nothing especially characteristic about it here.

Pluto is located at Sun/Moon's Node (desire to compel others, seeking to influence the masses, sharing a common and mass fate) = Mercury/Node (desire for spiritual and mental supremacy over others) = Sun/Saturn (inhibitions in development, serious handicaps) = Saturn/Node (sacrificing oneself for others, suffering because of others, common suffering) = Moon/Mars (one-sidedness, fanaticism) = Moon/Jupiter (desire for popularity, attainment of the respect and good thoughts of many). If we transfer these interpretations, which have been quoted almost verbatim from *The*

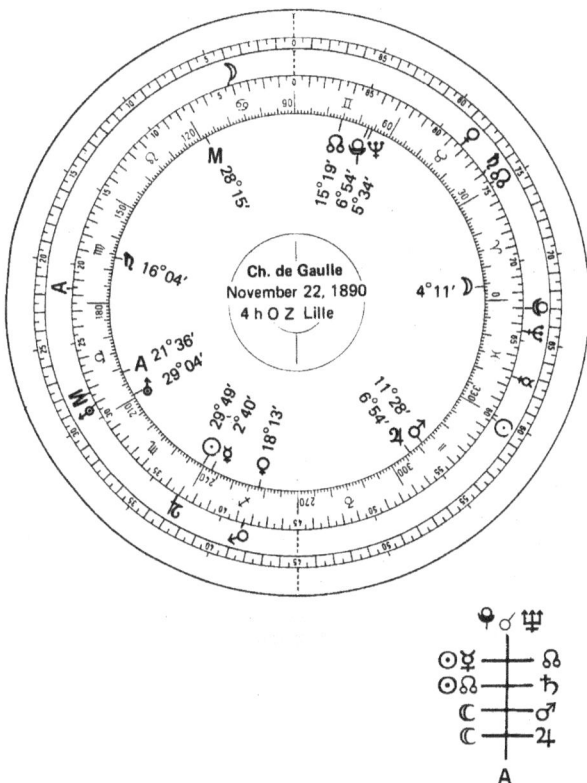

*Figure 15*

*Combination of Stellar Influences*, they are in agreement with DeGaulle's life.

When both positive and negative configurations are contained in such a structural picture, as a rule the favorable configurations are triggered by favorable transits and the negative ones by negative transits. In 1968 (Figure 16) there were two crises: Saturn transited the complex of Neptune-Ascendant-Pluto. France was shaken by revolt, when half a million people went on strike, and DeGaulle was compelled to make an unscheduled return from a trip. On May 24, he threatened to resign, and on May 25, there was

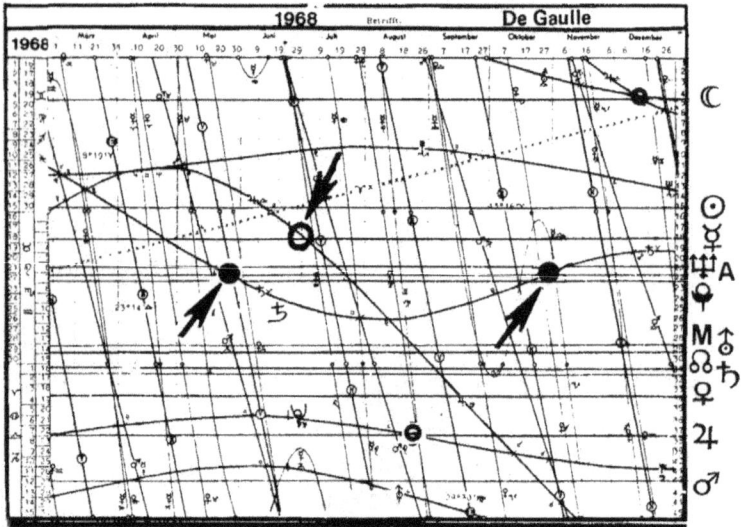

*Figure 16*

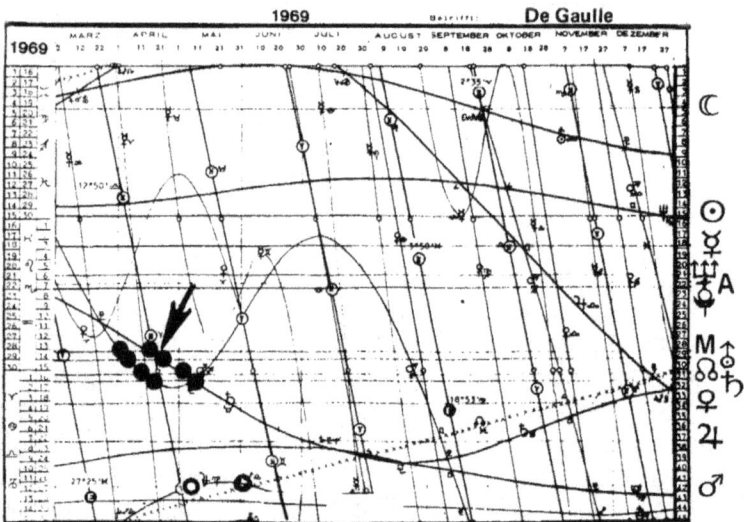

*Figure 17*

barricade fighting in Paris and further strikes broke out in Paris. There were even posters that stated: "Hang De Gaulle!" At the end of June, as Jupiter transited the position line of Mercury, the absolute majority cast a favorable vote for DeGaulle. Pluto was approaching Jupiter for the second time, and DeGaulle was thus able to retain power.

In November, France was confronted with a finance and currency crisis. However, the franc was not devaluated after all, due to West German support.

In 1968, I stated: "A severe and vital crisis is possible in April 1969, when Mars and Saturn transit the Midheaven, Uranus, and Saturn. Of possible aid to him could be Jupiter over Mars in his attempt to overcome this crisis. Nevertheless, he will remain without any chances and will steadily lose his prestige. . . ."

DeGaulle threatened to resign on April 10, 1969, and demanded a plebiscite, with the result that fifty-two percent voted in DeGaulle's disfavor. On April 28, Poher, the president of the senate, became preliminary head of the government. Corresponding to DeGaulle's defeat was the positioning of the Saturn transit and Mars in perigee in the same place.

De Gaulle died November 9, 1970. Here, too, it is very easy to find the corresponding positions in the graphic ephemeris. Saturn was crossing over the Moon, which in this case can be taken to mean separation from the people. Of significance is, however, the transit of Neptune over the Sun, which in the radix is at the midpoint of Mars and Saturn, the so-called death axis. Because of this configuration, the imminence of death is unmistakable.

Let us now take a look at the directions. Progressed Saturn is at 15 Virgo 29 in a square to the Node at 15 Gemini 19. This indicates separation (Saturn) from the community (Moon's Node). Pluto, advanced by measure of the solar arc to 28 Leo 14, is located here in an exact square to the death-axis Mars/Saturn at 28 Scorpio 46. Using a small orb, we can find further critical directions, such as

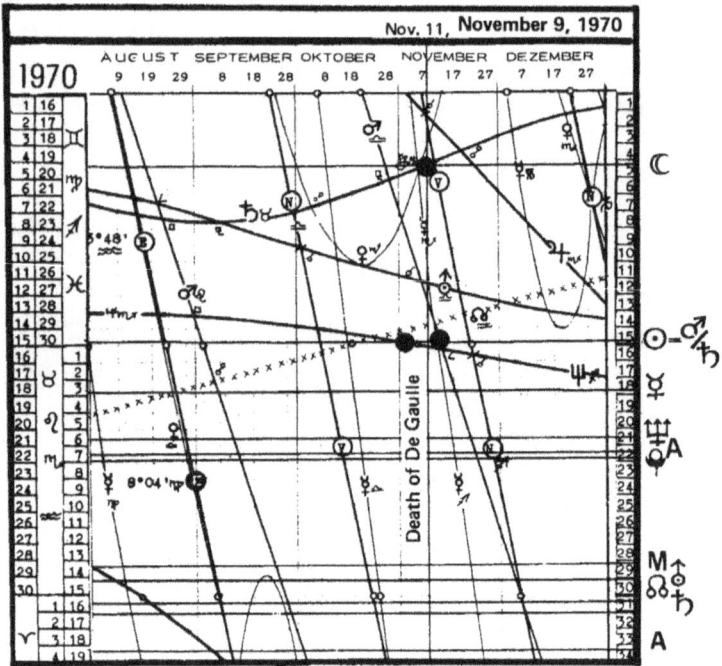

*Figure 18*

Uranus at 20 Sagittarius 24 sesquiquadrate Neptune, and Saturn at 7 Sagittarius 24 had already gone through the opposition to Pluto.

This clearly demonstrates how prognostications can be made using only the graphic ephemerides.

Chapter 5

# Setting Up an Election Forecast

It is not easy to make a correct election forecast weeks or even months beforehand, especially when a configuration such as Jupiter semisquare Neptune, which is particularly evocative of incorrect prognostication, is due. Of prime importance is that the prognosticator take care to evaluate the configurations objectively. Another prerequisite is the comparison with a larger number of persons. A cursory and off-hand investigation can easily result in a false prognostication.

Our investigation is concerned with the West German election in September 1969. In my monthly surveys I often noticed Pluto approaching Jupiter in the fall of 1969, in the cases of both Franz Joseph Strauss and Karl Schiller. I concluded from this, especially due to the fact that the time set for the election was not known as yet, that is was entirely possible for these two ministers, each a member of the two traditionally opposing parties, to continue to work together.

After the time of election had been set, I made a general survey of the politicians involved. I found the following contrast: in August, the orbits of Saturn and Pluto in the case of Schiller struck Saturn, and the Midheaven with Strauss. This could only lead to the conclusion that any kind of cooperation between the two ministers appeared to be impossible and that in fact the differences

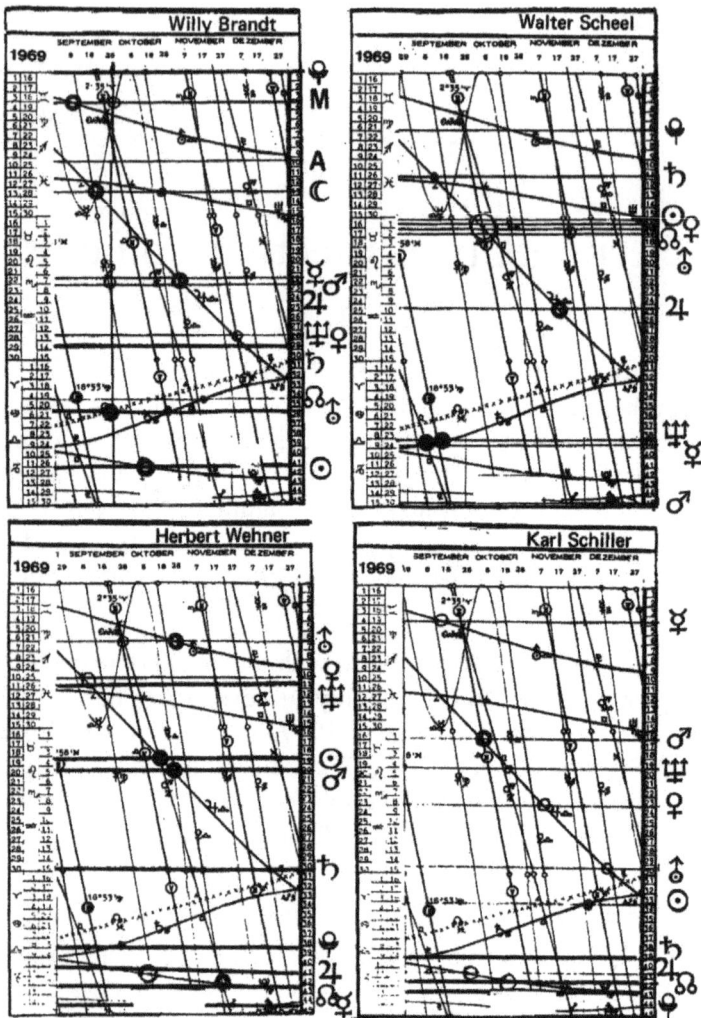

*Figure 19*

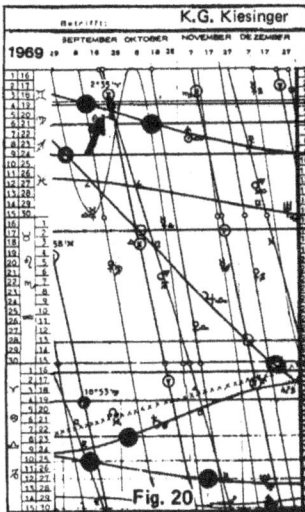

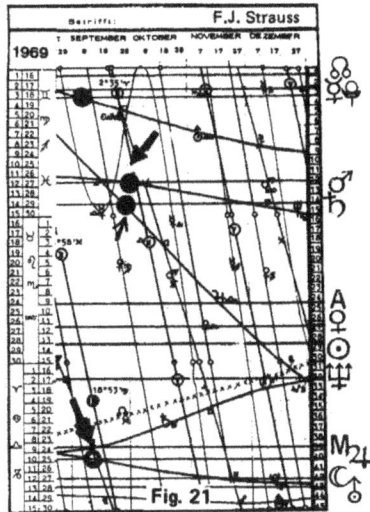

*Figure 20*

would widen. It was obvious that Strauss' success configuration would come at the beginning of September (Figure 20) when he did indeed receive a great deal of attention and response due to his speeches. Subsequently, however, Saturn approached the Midheaven (difficulties, failure), and Uranus transited Pluto (upset, tension). This involved unpleasant clashes with the young revolutionists. At the time of the election Neptune transited Mars (paralysis, disappointment, illness), and Jupiter transited Saturn (vexation, trouble). This means, therefore, that prospects at the time of election were very poor.

Things looked completely different in Schiller's case, who always showed confidence. The critical situation in August is expressed here also in the transits of Saturn and Pluto over Saturn. At this point, however, Pluto approached the complex of Node, Jupiter, and Pluto—the success configuration in this particular radix. The due date was somewhere between the end of September and the middle of October. At the same time, Jupiter transited Mars, and in contrast, transited Saturn in the case of Strauss. It could therefore be presumed that Schiller had better prospects for the election than did Strauss.

The more important question, however, was that of whether Kurt Kiesinger would retain the office of chancellor. On examining the annual diagram, there are many black dots, i.e., negative points. In September, Uranus first transited the illness-axis Saturn/Neptune. Since the same constellation was due in the spring when he had to undergo an operation on his jaw, there was reason for supposing that he could become ill or be exposed to extra stress and strain. The transits of Sun, Mars, and Mercury over the Moon around the election date gave no indication at all of any great success in the offing. Mars over Jupiter was to bring about decisions at the beginning of October. I also calculated the significant directions: progressed Mars (3 Cancer 23) conjunction Neptune (3 Cancer 17) sesquiquadrate Saturn (18 Aquarius 39) pointed to a lack of energy, failures, paralyzed activity, and vain efforts. These directions were stimulated by transiting Uranus. Jupiter opposition Sun in the middle of October was too weak to produce any notable momentum.

Since party leaders, Kiesinger and Strauss, had no good prospects, then there must have been favorable configurations for those of the opposing party.

I had noted many years before that in the case of Willy Brandt, progressed Jupiter conjunction Uranus would become due around 1969, meaning advancement for him at that time. We see in the annual diagram that Pluto approached the Sun. This configuration was due in October and indicates power of assertion and a striving for power. I do not know Willy Brandt's exact time of birth, but the solar position should be fairly correct. The Midheaven could shift by about a degree, in which case the transits of Uranus, Sun, and Mars over the Midheaven would have been due on the day of election. Jupiter over Moon at the end of the month led to an increase in his popularity, which consequentially meant more votes. After the middle of October, Saturn over Uranus could indicate the sudden arise of problems, and Neptune over the Moon could dampen the public esteem. At the beginning of November, the success complex Mars-Mercury-Jupiter was transited by Jupiter.

Brandt's success is very strongly dependent on his party strategist, Herbert Wehner. In his annual diagram, we see Pluto approaching Jupiter, thus meaning the presence of an unusual success configuration. Nonetheless, Saturn over Pluto and Jupiter over Neptune can only be termed negative. In October, Jupiter over Sun and Mars are counted as positive.

Walter Scheel's annual diagram was of particular interest. Up to the end of September, it was negative in tone due to Saturn and Pluto over Neptune, Neptune over Saturn, and Jupiter over Saturn. But at the beginning of October, Jupiter transited the complex of Sun, Venus, Uranus, and Node. Brandt and Wehner have this Jupiter configuration in common, this making success likely. What could not be foreseen was the odd way in which this was to come about.

This was my prognostication: Jupiter semisquare Neptune indicates incorrect forecasts at this time. One can see from the axis Jupiter/Neptune = Saturn/Node that there can be great difficulties in the way of partners coming to terms, or that the one partner will feel disappointed, injured, or cheated by the other. The lunar eclipse together with Mars and Uranus indicates incidents, demonstrations, unrest (316 injured during the election campaign, of these 124 were civilians and 192 were police officers).

These configurations now have to be correlated with the cosmograms of the politicians involved. At the time of election, the incumbent chancellor, Kurt Kiesinger, was most likely not in the best of health, and his situation could be considered only in a slightly favorable light. The direction of Mars to Neptune can mean at the very least a severe disappointment or susceptibility to disease.

F.J. Strauss showed a great deal of pre-election activity. Neptune over Mars and Jupiter over Saturn at the end of September could lead to disappointment. With von Hassel, Benda, Katzer, and Schroder, other prominent members of the Union, there are ample negative influences present, lending credence to the presumption that the party would not achieve its goal. Walter Scheel would have many difficulties to deal with before the election, but successes after election day are not unlikely.

Subsequent to the election, where there was no clear majority, Scheel join forces with Brandt and a new coalition was formed. Willy Brandt thus became the new chancellor.

There are many other examples we can take from politics where prognostications based on the graphic ephemerides have been made and substantiated. In order, however, to give this book greater variety and scope, the following pages will present the successes and failures of individuals, and then various diseases and other aspects of life.

## Chapter 6

# The Five-million Pound
# Train Robbery

On August 8, 1963, a British postal train was robbed. The take was five million pounds sterling. One of the leaders of the band was Ronald Biggs. According to the information given by various journalists and commentators, he was born August 8, 1930 (see Figure 21).

The hour of birth is not known, but one of the great merits of the graphic ephemerides is that a prognostication is possible even without knowledge of the birth time if one knows enough about the person in question and his or her circumstances.

One would expect to find here certain correspondences to Mars, Pluto (violence), Jupiter (successful enterprise), and Saturn (separation, escape, travel). This is indeed the case. However, there are not many hints to be found among the traditional aspects. Clearer indications can be had in the cosmogram from the mid-point combinations in the 90° circle; for example, Mars = Sun/Pluto: Extraordinary ambition, overstrain, ruthlessness.

Before making a prognostication on the basis of the graphic ephemeris, it is always a good idea to take a close look at the natal chart and to note the most important structural elements. Hence, alongside the cosmogram we may also make use of a listing of the

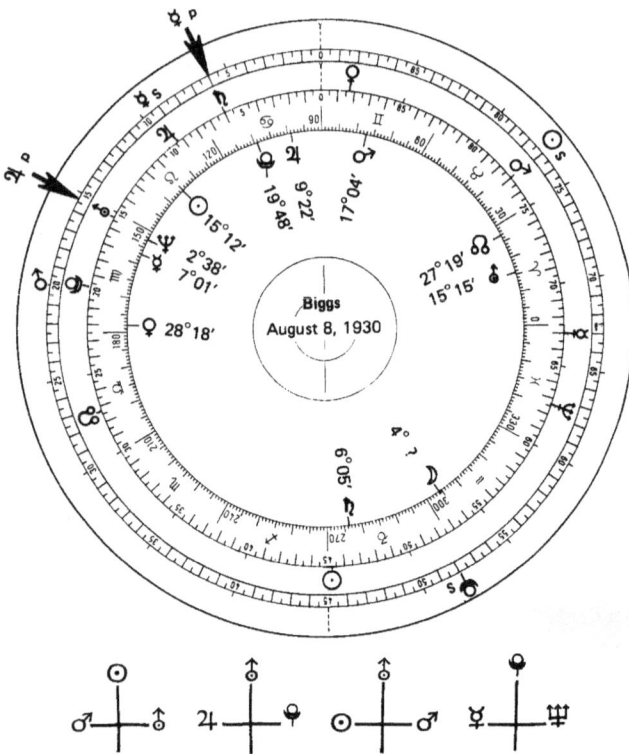

*Figure 21*

various midpoint relationships. The following are the most pre-
dominant configurations:

PL = ME/NE: Unusual acts, placing great demands on one's nervous energy, an actor.

SO = MA/UR: Capability of sudden increase in physical energy,
person capable of quick action.

UR= SO/MA: Impulsive action, exceeding the limits of one's energies, and in criminal cases, arrest.

UR= JU/PL: Fanatical striving for reform, quick grasp of any situation, successful organization.

These are the configurations that have to be substantiated by the events. At the time of the robbery, the solar arc was 31° 50′. Adding this to Mars, we get solar arc Mars at 18 Cancer 54, almost conjunct Pluto. Together with Pluto = Mercury/Neptune this results in thinking directed toward one's goal, rich imagination (ingenuity), the realization of plans, acting on consideration and from experience.

Mercury + Solar arc = 38° 51′ = 8 Libra 51, i.e., square Jupiter = Venus/ Pluto = Sun/Neptune: success, unusual good luck, success without any special effort.

Sun + solar arc = 17 Libra 52 - 90 - Mars 17 Gemini 04 = Sun/Pluto = Mercury/Venus: overcoming difficulties and danger through unusual energy and effort. On transcribing the positions from the natal chart to the graphic ephemeris for 1963, we immediately notice one very particular configuration. This is the aspect of Jupiter and Uranus that coincides with natal Pluto. One might object that this configuration is due for a great number of persons having Pluto in this position, but in this case, Pluto is located in the natal chart at the midpoint Mercury/Neptune, as ascertained previously, and which points to unusual acts, high demands made on nervous energy, and acting talent. This configuration, therefore, is given individual coloring through Mercury/Neptune. In addition, the Moon's Node comes to meet this configuration in the graphic ephemeris, with the Node in combination with Jupiter and Uranus indicating joint, sudden good luck or some special success. If Biggs' birth-time were known, one could certainly apply some personal points as well. One unfavorable aspect is that in the lower part of the ephemeris showing Neptune transiting Venus at the end of August, which can be considered an undermining or denial of love life. He did indeed become separated from his wife due to his imprisonment. In addition, a series of critical Mars aspects over Uranus, Neptune, and Pluto appears from the middle of August onward, and this is therefore probably the time at which he was arrested.

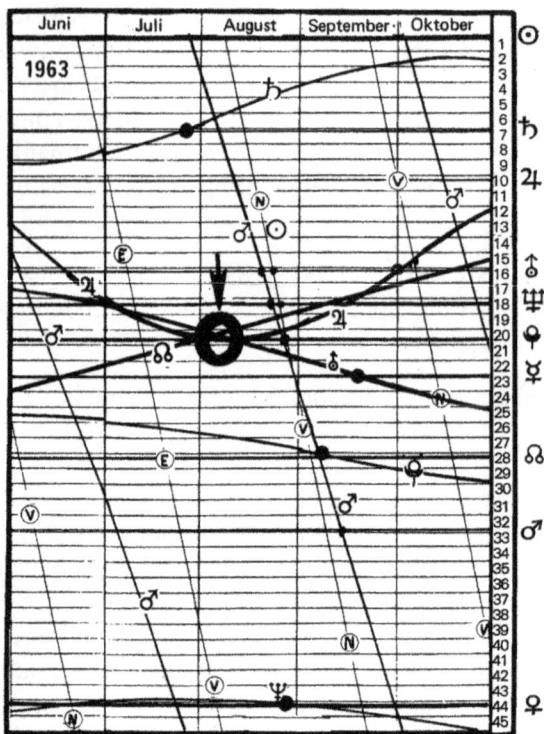

*Figure 22*

The midpoint Jupiter/Pluto transited the solar position at the beginning of August (Figures 22 and 23), indicating sudden good luck, i.e., in combination with the solar position. However, the midpoint Saturn/Neptune was approaching the Sun, and this tends to limit good luck. The robber succeeded in escaping after spending two years in prison and roamed the world before spending all the money.

This example demonstrates how success in many fields of enterprise can be read from the graphic ephemeris. It has also been shown that on this basis any number of persons can be observed and their possible successes or failures mapped for the future. If,

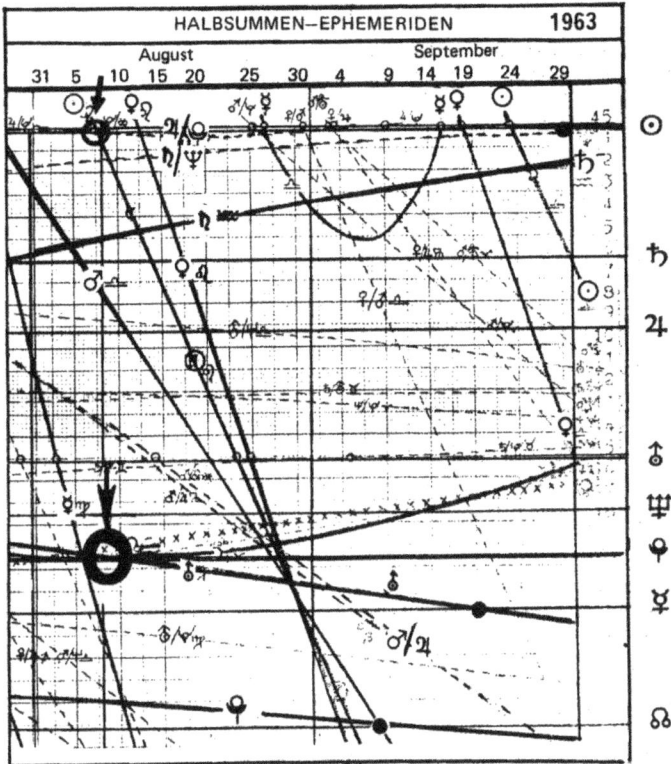

*Figure 23*

for example, there is knowledge of a particular crime being planned, one could under circumstances set the date for its possible execution, and it is also possible to determine when a certain criminal has poor constellations due, in which case there might be an increased chance at that time to capture him.

Chapter 7

# The Calculation of a Birth

The advance calculation of a birth is not at all easy, but with the aid of the graphic ephemeris we are able to survey a greater span of time. However, one must remain aware of the fact that the problem cannot be solved by transits alone; directions also have to be taken into account.

This case concerns a female birth on May 6, 1923, at 4:55 a.m. at 51N00, 6E46. The mother, Inge Lehmann, was age twenty-seven when she married. She gave birth to a child two years later that due to a blood-group incompatibility (rhesus factor) did not develop normally and is today still in a home. The father died when the child was age four. The mother hesitated until her thirty-eighth year before she could decide to remarry. Her second husband was not in particularly good health, but nevertheless he wanted a child and stated: "A marriage without any children just isn't a marriage." His wife was above all afraid of complications such as those that had occurred with her first child, and she was somewhat late in years for a pregnancy. On closely examining the natal chart, I noticed that in the 1965-1966, progressed Mars would transit Venus. On the date of birth in 1966, progressed Mars was at 11 Cancer 59, and accordingly it must have formed the exact square to Venus in the year 1965. As we know, this aspect of Venus and Mars is decisive for all matters of love and, above all, for conception and birth. No time was to be lost since she was now

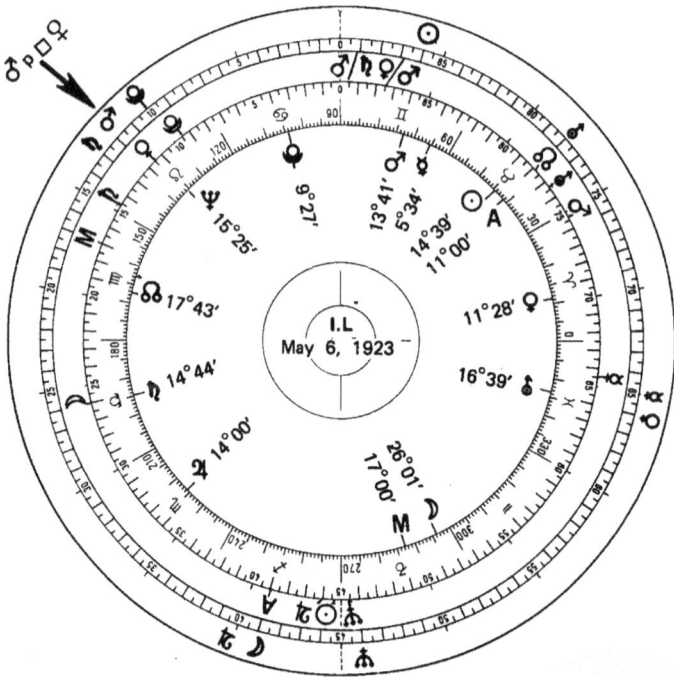

*Figure 24*

already past the age forty, and every opportunity had to be taken. We see in the figure the stellar positions in progression entered in the outer circle. The transit of Mars over Venus, top left, is very striking (Figure 24). In addition, in the outer circle we find Jupiter approaching the Ascendant, where the progressed Moon was located. The progressed Sun was approaching the midpoint Venus/Mars, which was opposite the complex of Jupiter, Sun, and Neptune.

Using the graphic 45° ephemeris for 1965 a possible time for conception had to be determined. The best opportunity seemed to be the Jupiter transit in September over its own position and the

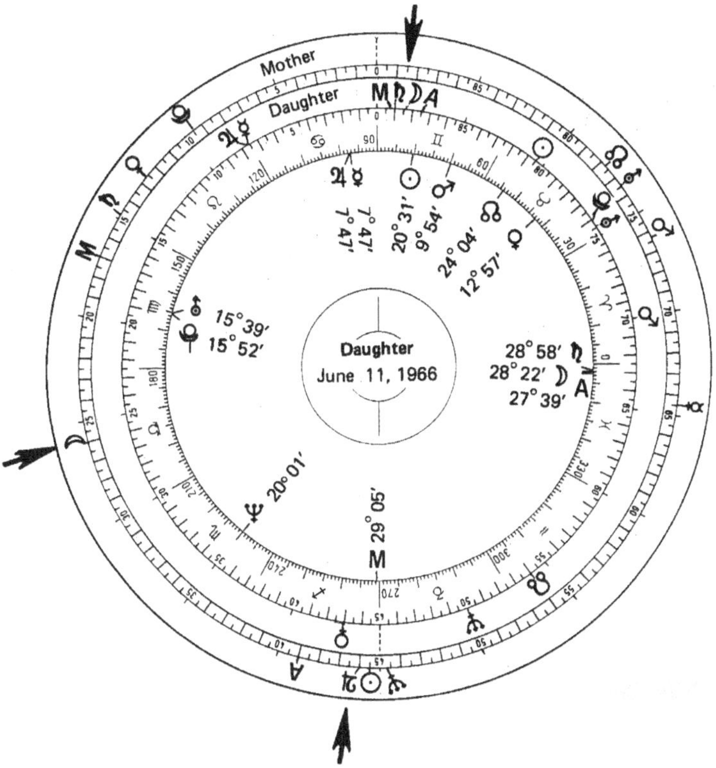

*Figure 25*

Sun, and in the days following, Sun and Venus also transited these points. We have already ascertained that the progressed Moon was approaching the Ascendant, and we find here that during this time the transiting Moon also crossed the Ascendant and Jupiter, together with Sun. It therefore would be possible for the progressed Moon to be triggered during this transit by the transiting Moon. There were other transits due at this time as well, such as the Sun and Venus over the Moon, Mars, and Uranus. In September, it was time for conception to take place since the coming months would see the very unfavorable Saturn aspect to the Moon. It was therefore recommended that the time around the beginning of September was best for a conception. She did become pregnant and it was

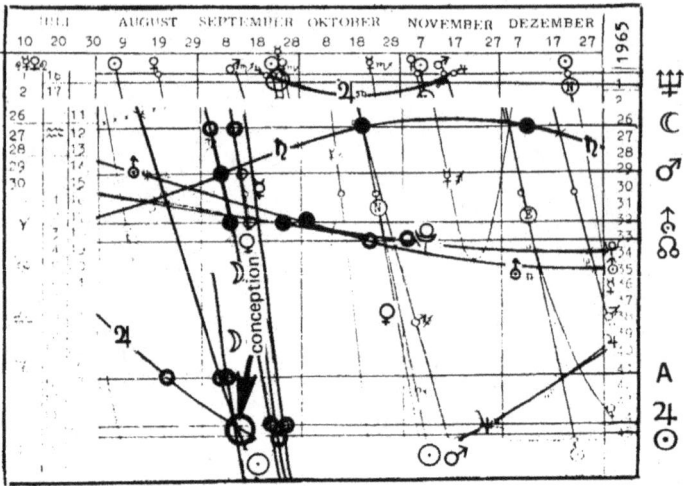

*Figure 26*

now necessary to calculate the probable date of birth, which should occur around the beginning of June 1966. Saturn aspected Jupiter and the Sun here, and the configuration of Jupiter and the Sun was also triggered about June 11 by Venus and the transiting Moon. It has frequently been observed that the natal Moon and conception Moon coincide. There was this possibility and indeed the birth occurred on June 1, 1966 at 11:10 p.m. The parents were overjoyed, and this was reflected by the transit of Jupiter over Pluto and Venus in the weeks subsequent to the birth.

Chapter 8

# The Correct Calculation of a Birth

Many births have been correctly calculated in advance. In this case, the mother was born December 1, 1945, at 10:30 p.m. in Bremen (Figure 27). The solar arc is 23° 38′. We find the following configurations in the outer 90° circle: solar arc Uranus-135-solar arc Venus, which is a frequently observed conception and birth constellation. Solar arc Jupiter-180-Midheaven means personal happiness or special success, and the Midheaven at Venus/Mars can also correspond to a felicitous birth. Progressed Venus was semisquare the Moon, which among other things can also apply to expectant mothers. At the same time, solar arc Pluto-45-Jupiter was at Venus/Uranus, pointing to a successful delivery.

It was known that the birth was supposed to occur at the beginning of March 1969. Looking at the graphic 45° ephemeris (Figure 28a), we see the direction solar arc Pluto = Jupiter = Venus/Uranus triggered by transiting Mars on the 9th. Transiting Mercury crossed Venus, and transiting Venus crossed the Sun and Saturn. The Sun's transit of Mars triggered the direction solar arc Venus-135-Mars.

This example clearly illustrates the interplay of directions and transits and how they should be combined.

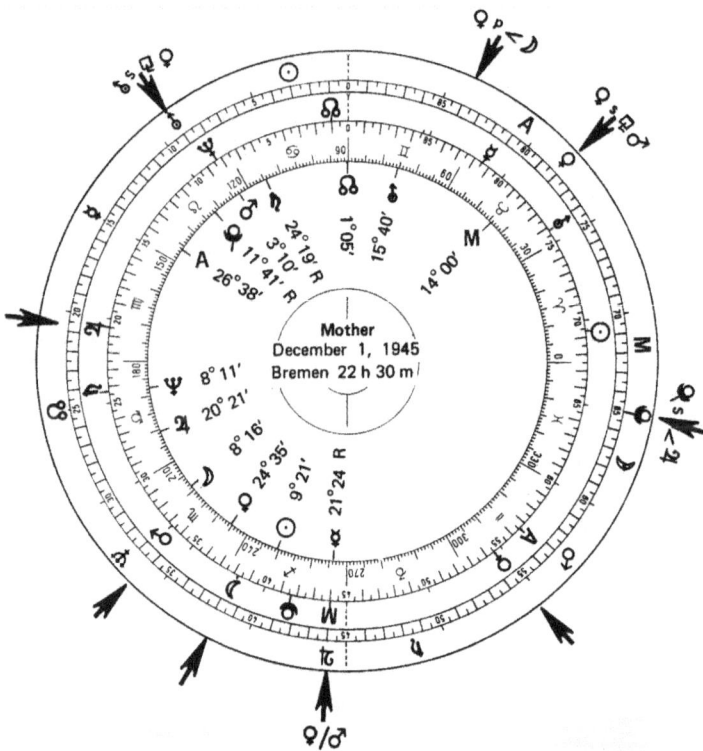

*Figure 27*

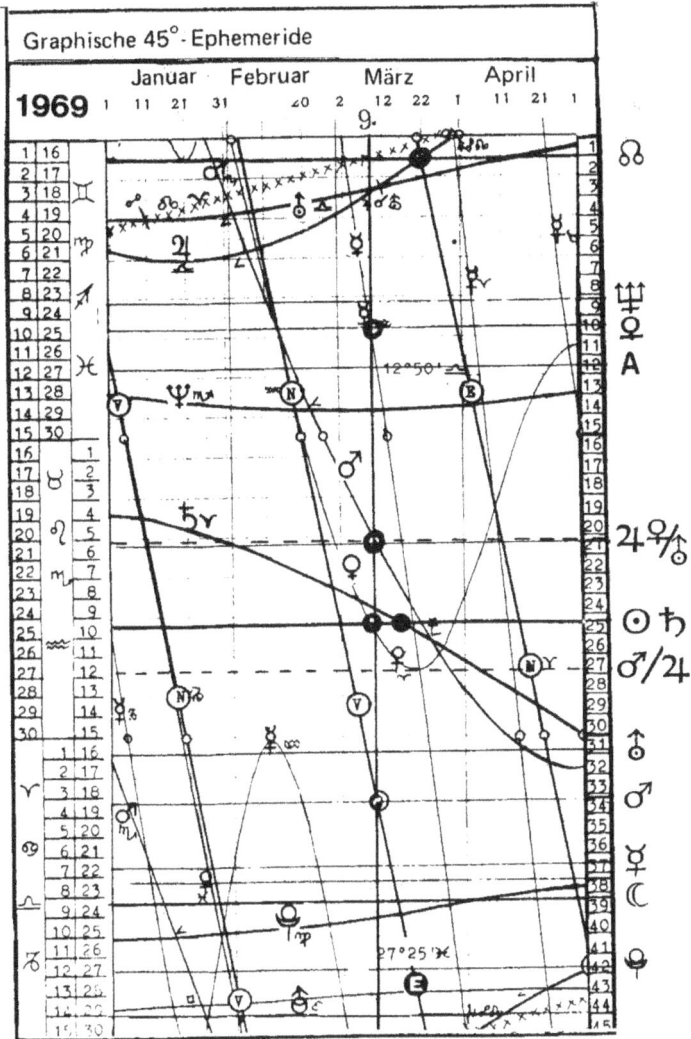

*Figure 28*

Chapter 9

# The Danger of False Prognostications

By no means should one assume that everything can be read and mapped by means of the graphic ephemerides. The importance of the directions and the fact of the transits acting more or less as triggering elements will be substantiated time and again. Returning to the example given in Figure 26, the first husband died four years after the birth of his child. In this same case, death recurs likewise in a child's fourth year, the death of the mother.

In the beginning of August 1970, I received the news that Inge had suffered a severe stroke on July 26, 1970, at 4:45 p.m. and was in critical condition. I was asked to examine the case and frankly state what I thought the prospects were. The graphic ephemeris (Figure 29) makes it evident that around July 26, first Mars and then Sun and Venus transited Uranus, which most certainly can allude to a stroke. Pluto was approaching the Ascendant, but this does not necessarily have to be considered especially critical. Of significance, however, is the transit of Neptune over Saturn, which was repeated in the fall of that year. This gives an idea of the severity of the attack.

In Inge's cosmogram at the time of the child's birth, progressed Mars aspected Venus, but in the years following it had been approaching Saturn. Experience has shown that an aspect of Mars

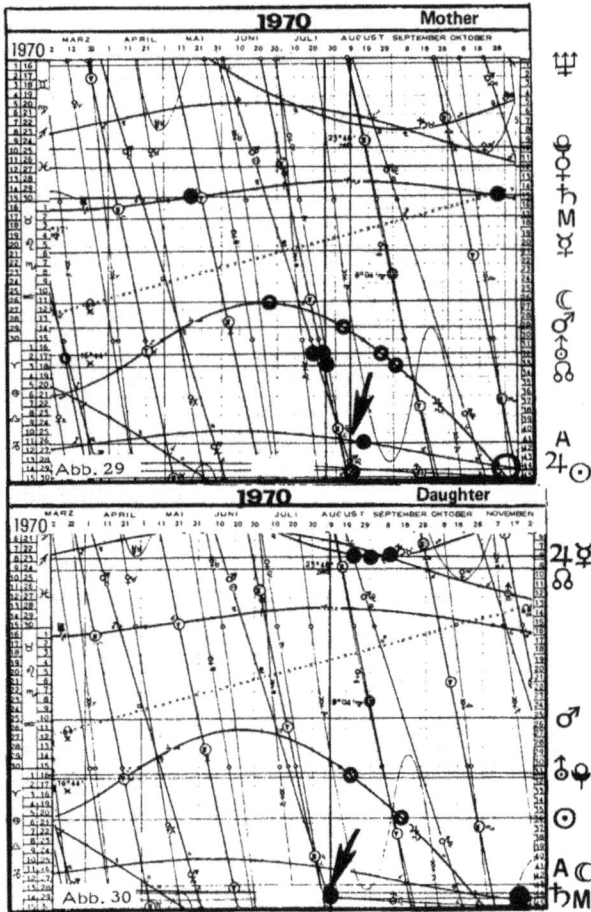

*Figure 29*

and Saturn always makes an appearance in times of death and hence can mean vital danger.

This made me recognize the gravity of the situation, and I did not quite know what I was to tell the husband. It was impossible to say that her death could possibly be expected within the next few days; after all, it might have been possible for her to overcome the crisis. Therefore, I wrote to him saying that the configuration of progressed Mars square Saturn could be considered a death configuration, but that there was hope of recovery in the event of the favorable Jupiter configurations over Mars, Uranus, and Moon's Node turning up in the near future. Also to be taken into account was the transit at the end of October of Jupiter together with Pluto over Jupiter and Sun, and that by then perhaps a recovery could be achieved.

However, in this case, Jupiter and the Sun are by no means favorably positioned because of their aspects to Neptune, located in the 360° circle exactly on the midpoint of Sun and Jupiter. In addition, the Sun and Jupiter are at the midpoint of Mars and Saturn, which is in itself indicative of death. It now depended on how the configuration on August 10 would resolve when Mars transited the Sun and Jupiter and the midpoint Mars/Saturn. It was negative. Inge's death came on August 10.

This example should serve as a warning against incautious prognostication. As can be seen, not everything is to be read from the configurations alone.

We discover in the annual diagram of the daughter (Figure 29) that transiting Mars crossed the complex of Moon, Saturn and Midheaven. This is the decisive point of contact, which was already ascertained at the birth of the child. In addition, Saturn and the Midheaven were in close conjunction at birth, and at age four, progressed Saturn had just transited the MC.

Chapter 10

# The Evolution of the
# Conception Cosmogram

Heinz Fidelsberger, M.D., head of the Viennese Astrological Society, carried out an experiment concerning cosmic twins. He discovered that on April 25, 1947, two boys were born at the same time to different mothers in the same maternity ward. Both boys, therefore, had the same cosmic natal chart. In addition, it was determined that both boys had the same weight and length at birth. In the course of time, however, differences did develop.

Of interest for the purpose of our investigation are the birth dates of the parents in relation to birth and conception. The two boys are Ernst and Ferdinand. The birth times for the parents is unknown to me, yet we will still be able to bring evidence of many coinciding configurations. The natal chart of the two natives is given in Figure 34. Figure 35 results from the transcription of the natal positions of the two mothers in the graphic ephemeris for the year 1947. Here, Ferdinand's mother's position lines are continuous, and those of Ernst's mother. are dotted. Our first discovery is that similar configurations are present with both mothers, i.e., in the first case Jupiter together with Mars are to be found in almost the same position as Jupiter and Venus in the second case. We may, therefore, assume that these configurations had some special influence on the births. This is in fact the case since Venus

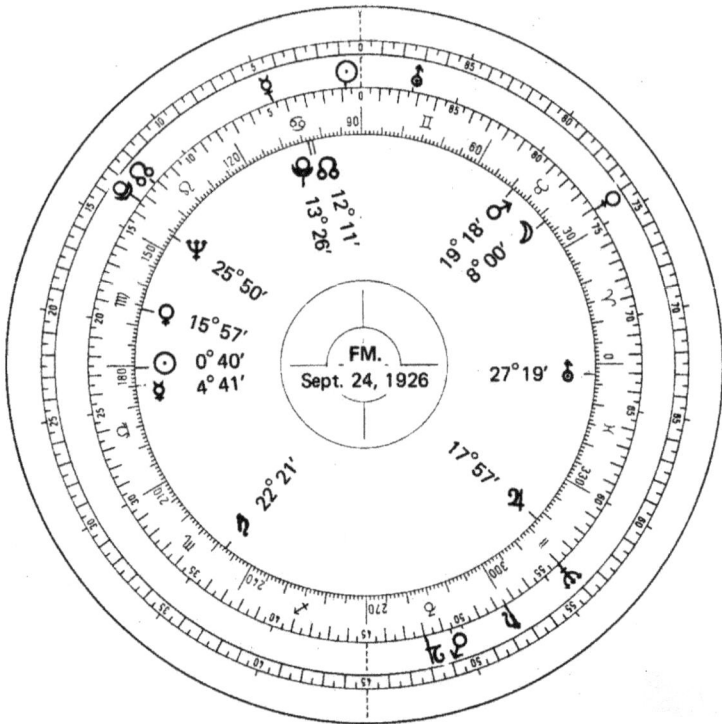

*Figure 30. Ferdinand's Mother*

transited this common point on April 25. Furthermore, we find Venus in Ferdinand's mother's, and the Sun in Ernst mother's coinciding. This configuration was jointly triggered by the transiting Sun. Finally, we discover the Uranus positions on almost the same spot, and these were jointly stimulated by transiting Venus. We must also make note of the fact there is an age difference of twelve years between the two women and that despite this, there is this concurrence of factors at the time of the births.

What we now need to find are the corresponding configurations at the time of conception. In general, the rule applies that the lunar position at the time of conception and at the time of birth is approx-

**Figure 31. Ferdinand**

imately the same. It is likely that conception came about at the end
of July 1946.

The transits of the Sun and Venus over the common position
lines of Ferdinand's mother's Venus and Ernst's mother's Sun become evident. These configurations indicate in particular the
physical (Sun) love (Venus). Another factor, however, is that the
Mars positions of the two husbands are at the same location and it
becomes clear that when Sun and Venus transit a woman's Venus
and a man's Mars, or the woman's Sun and the man's Mars,
conception can take place.

*Figure 32. Ernst's Mother*

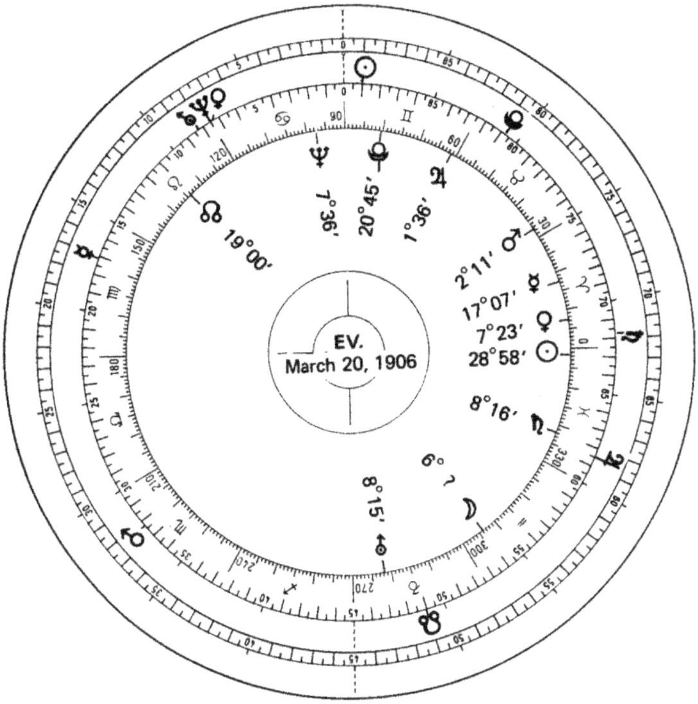

*Figure 33. Ernst*

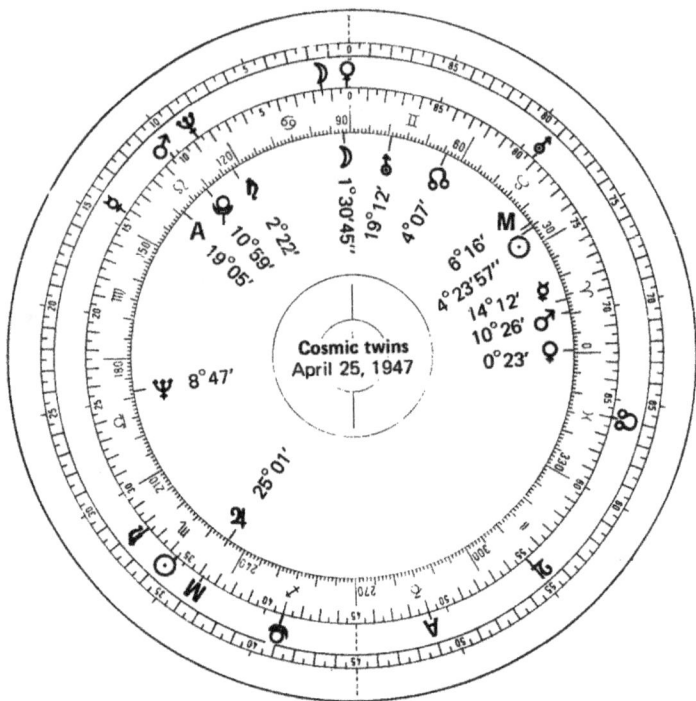

*Figure 34*

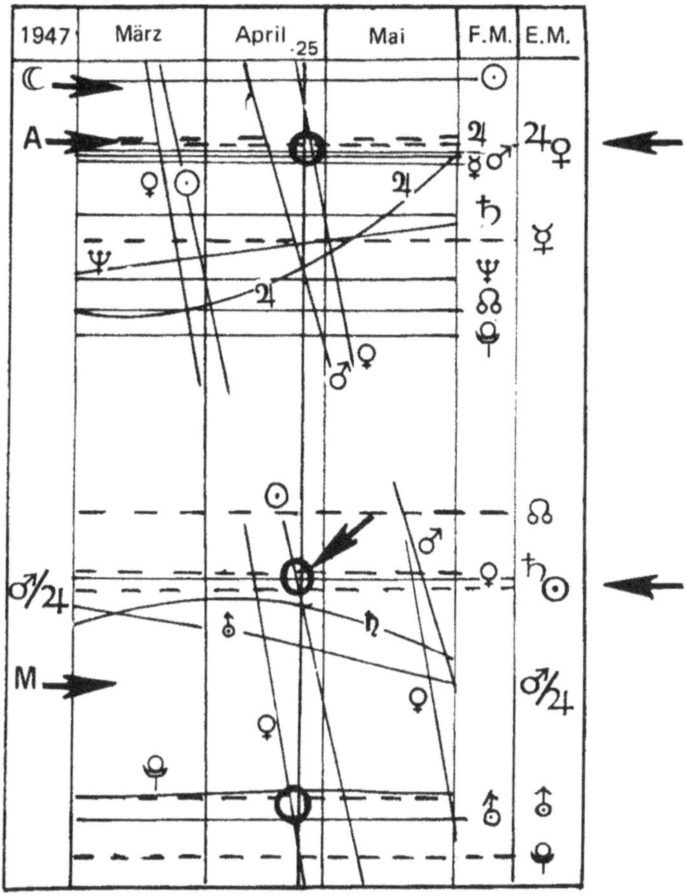

*Figure 35*

Chapter 11

# The Period of Pregnancy in the Graphic Ephemeris

The graphic ephemeris can be of particular aid in the event of pregnancy, making it possible to take precautions in the case of critical configurations, such as keeping to a certain diet and restricting the indulgence in certain substances such as caffeine, alcohol, etc., on the one hand, and on the other, to make the best use of the positive configurations. We had the opportunity to make a study of one woman's pregnancy which ended in the birth of a deformed child due to Thalidomide. The mother was born June 27, 1935, at 11:45 p.m. in Saarbruecken. The natal chart is presented in Figure 37.

The birth in question took place October 12, 1961, at 6:00 a.m. in Saarbruecken. The solar arc for this birth was at that time 25°04', and looking at the figure, we see that Saturn had just reached the solar position at the time of the birth, which cannot be considered to be very favorable, especially since Neptune had just transited this point. A responsible parent, one who knows something of cosmobiology, would never have chosen this time for conception. Figure 39 shows the transcription of the mother's natal picture to the graphic ephemeris. Since the child was born October 12, 1961, we can presume that conception occurred around the beginning of January, most likely as Mars transited the position lines

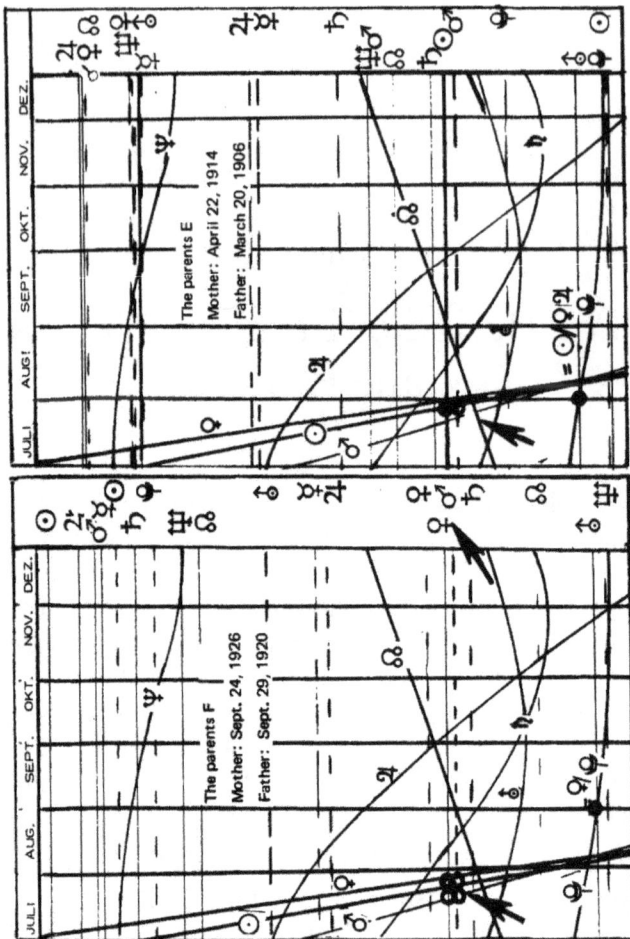

**Figure 36**

of Sun and Venus. This configuration was strengthened by a transit of Jupiter over Mars and Moon. Very critical configurations can be found to have formed already in February. As we have already seen from the directions, the direction of Saturn and Neptune approached the Sun. And here Jupiter and Saturn transited the posi-

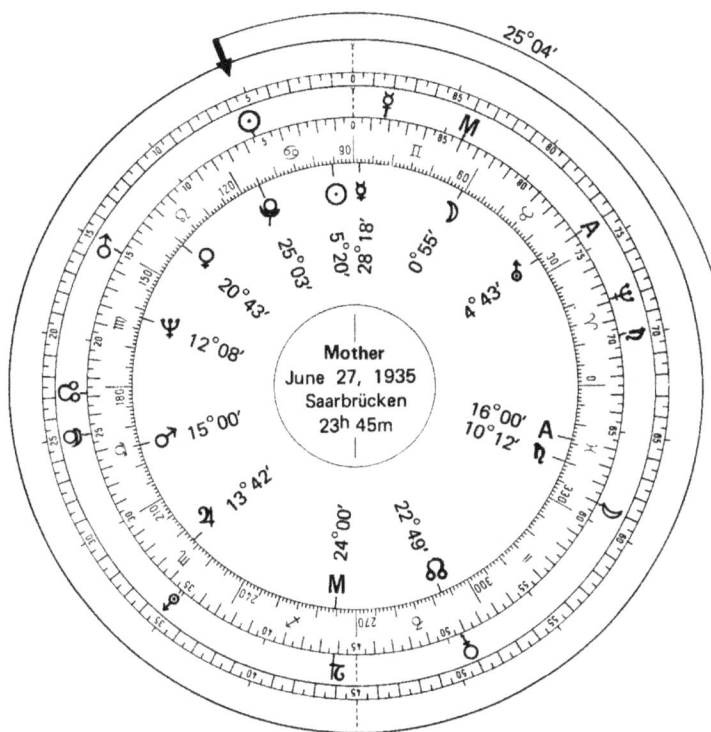

*Figure 37*

tion lines of Saturn and Pluto and, later on, Neptune as well. As has been researched, the effects of Thalidomide are manifested particularly between the twenty-fifth and forty-fourth day of pregnancy, which means the period from the middle of February to the beginning of March. One does not need to be an expert to see the correlation between the accumulation of critical configurations and the potential effects of the drug. Jupiter and Saturn practically collide with the illness-axis Saturn/Neptune. Therefore, there was great probability that the mother would become ill and need to take some medicine. Crucial in this case was the wrong choice of medication. Of significance in this connection is Neptune in the vicinity of the Midheaven so that the personality itself is affected.

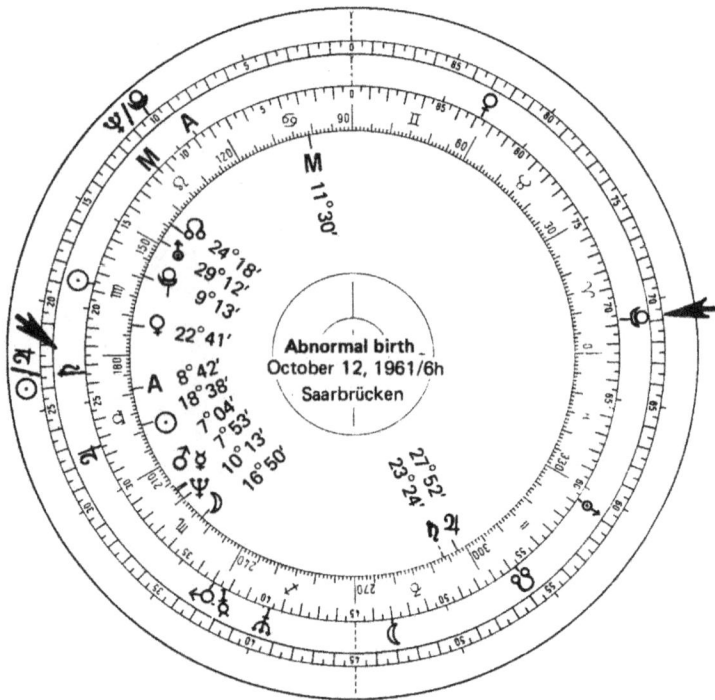

*Figure 38*

In the last few months prior to the birth, transiting Saturn and Pluto approached the critical position lines of Saturn and Pluto. Transiting Jupiter aspected Neptune, and transiting Neptune aspected the Midheaven and Mercury. This is, therefore, much the same configuration as in the spring. The birth took place during the New Moon of October 12, and it is likely that conception took place just before a New Moon. I have observed that similar factors and symptoms made their appearance even if they were not of such grave consequence as in the case of Thalidomide users that led to certain abnormalities. In the case of the Thalidomide children, heliocentric configurations in particular were present, in which significant planets were located at the midpoints of Earth/Saturn.

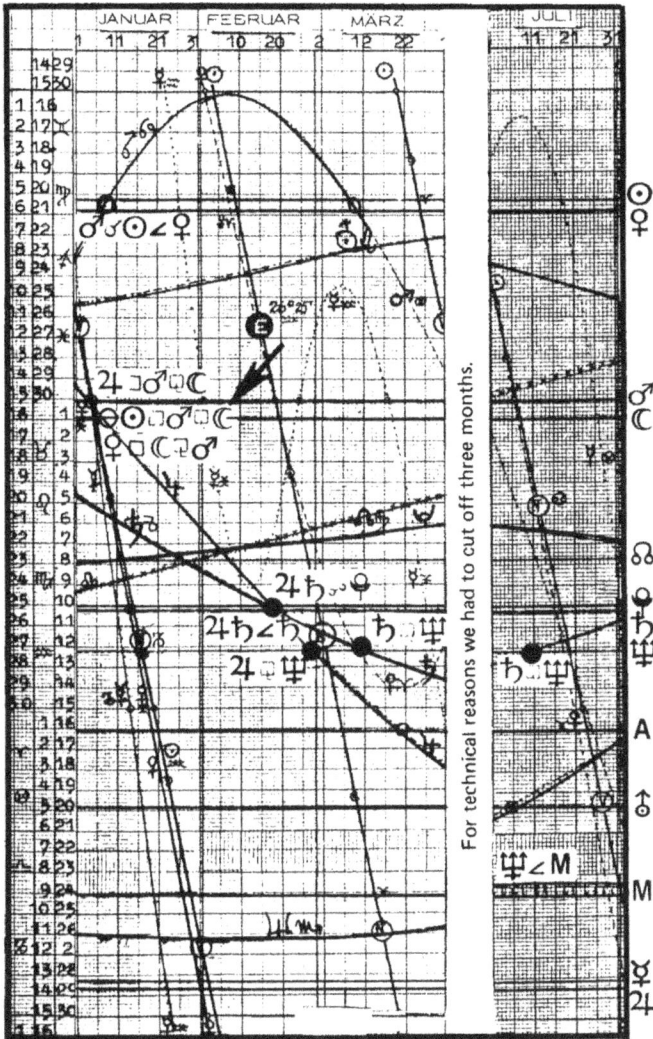

*Figure 39*

63

# Chapter 12

# Illness During Pregnancy

A woman who was born February 20, 1934, in Berlin, became pregnant in 1966. In August she suffered from an inflammation of the abdominal veins, and apparently had not been given the correct treatment from the start. On August 19, 1966, she was admitted to the hospital, and on October 21, it became necessary to induce birth. She was unconscious during delivery. The child was born October 21 at 10:20 p.m.

Crucial directions were due for the year 1966: solar arc Mars-45-Sun = Saturn/Neptune = Mars/Saturn, i.e., a critical illness configuration. Solar arc Venus-90-Neptune = Saturn/MC = Moon/MC, also a very grave direction. Solar arc MC-90-Venus, the configuration of birth. But even leaving aside the directions, a crisis in the summer months is immediately evident in the annual diagram when transiting Neptune aspected MC and Saturn.

However, there was compensation in the form of some favorable Jupiter transits over Sun, Ascendant, Jupiter, Uranus and Mars. At the time of birth there was Jupiter-135-Mercury. Since conception probably took place in January, we find here the transits of Jupiter, Venus, and Sun over the natal Venus, which would mean the strong physical attraction of one partner to the other.

The delivery took place under complete narcosis, typical of transiting Sun over Neptune, whereas a surgical delivery corre-

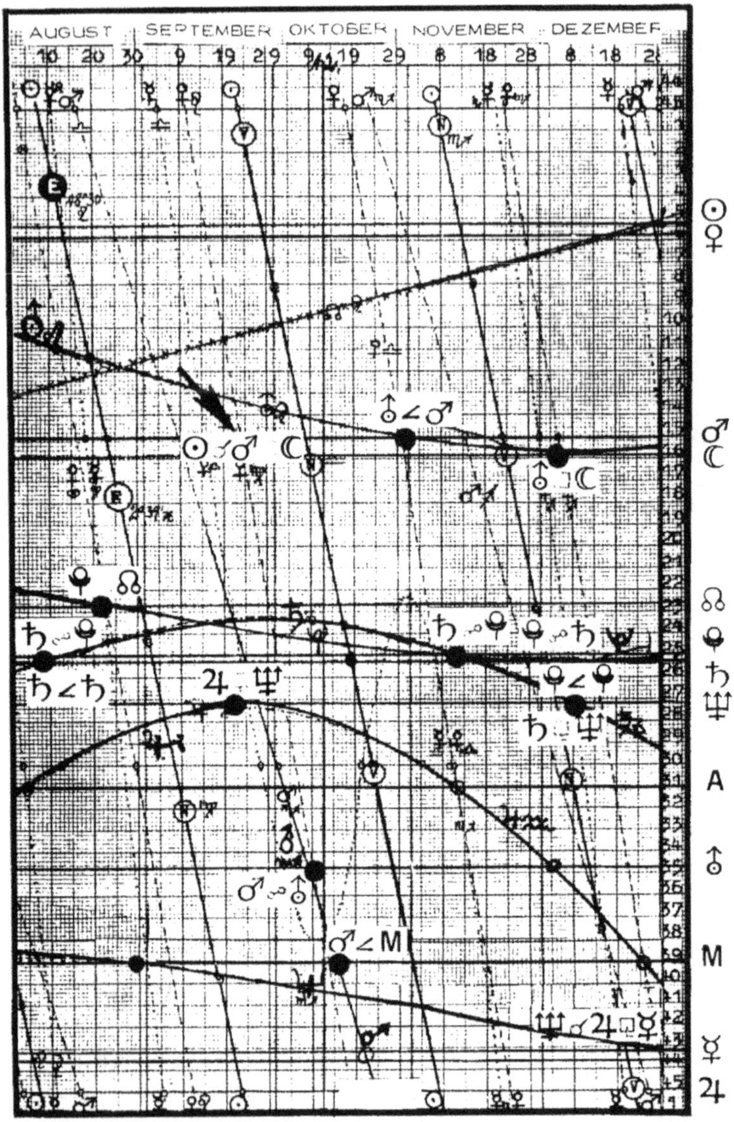

*Figure 40*

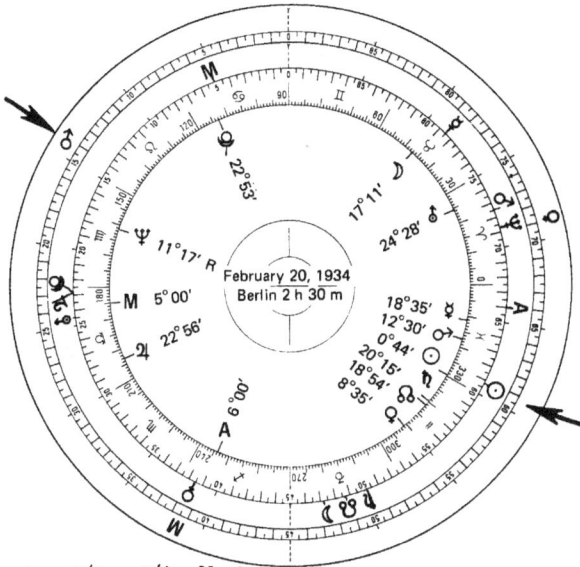

$\hbar = \odot/\varphi = \delta/\text{\textbf{\^{o}}} = M = \mathcal{D}$

$\mathcal{D} = \delta/\text{♀} = \delta/\text{4} = \Psi/\text{♀} = \text{\textbf{\^{o}}}/\Psi = \text{4}/\Psi$

$\text{♀} = \delta/M$

$\text{\textbf{\^{o}}} = \odot/\text{♉}$

$\text{☿} = \odot/M$

$\delta \, \mathcal{o}^o \, \Psi = \hbar/M$

$\Psi = \mathcal{D}/M = \hbar/M$

$\odot = \hbar/\Psi = \delta/\hbar = \text{\textbf{\^{o}}}/M$

**Figure 41**

sponds to Sun over Mars. Venus over Jupiter indicates the joy of the mother. In the period after the birth, difficulties are in evidence due to Saturn and transiting Uranus combined with Venus.

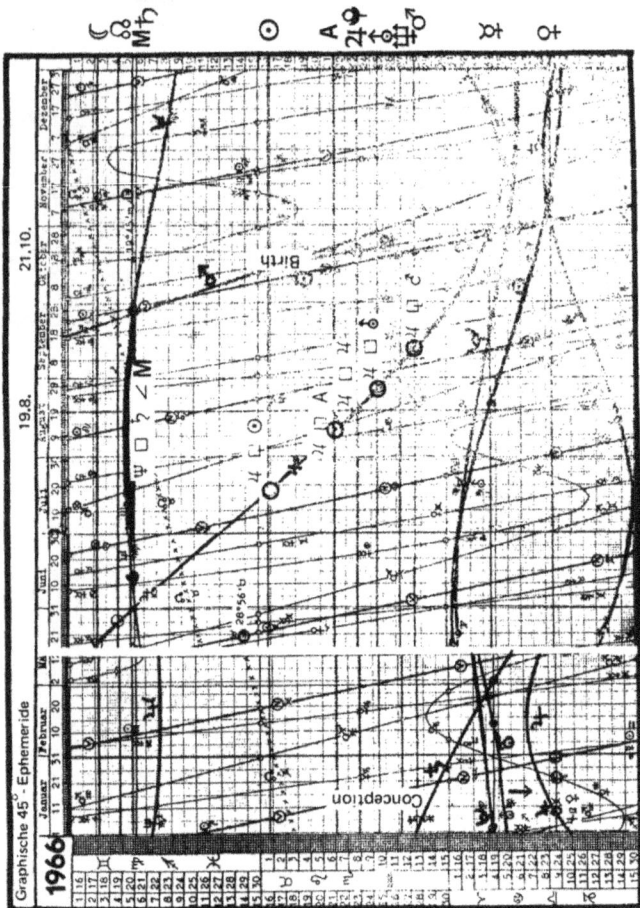

*Figure 42*

68

Chapter 13

# How to Find the
# Best Day for a Marriage

It is the desire of every couple in love to be truly happy on the day their marriage takes place. However, this does not always turn out to be the case. I can recall one case where the mother of the bride died just a few days before the day of the wedding. Since all the preparations had been completed and a number of relations were to come from far away, a postponement of the wedding was no longer possible, and grief overshadowed any joy one may have felt. Illness and mishap can also play a role in making a postponement necessary. Therefore, it is correct to take the precaution of looking through the annual diagrams of the individuals involved and to set the date for the wedding accordingly.

At the fairy tale wedding of Crown Princess Margarete of Denmark and Prince Hendrik, the bride gave the impression of being very happy. And this indeed corresponds to the configurations.

The outer 90° circle of the princess contains the solar arc directions (Figure 43), and among these is solar arc Jupiter over the Moon, pointing to a happy (Jupiter) woman (Moon). Located opposite are Venus and solar arc Mars, which, in combination with the Moon and Jupiter, can mean marital felicity.

Solar arc Uranus at the Midheaven opposition Pluto is primar-

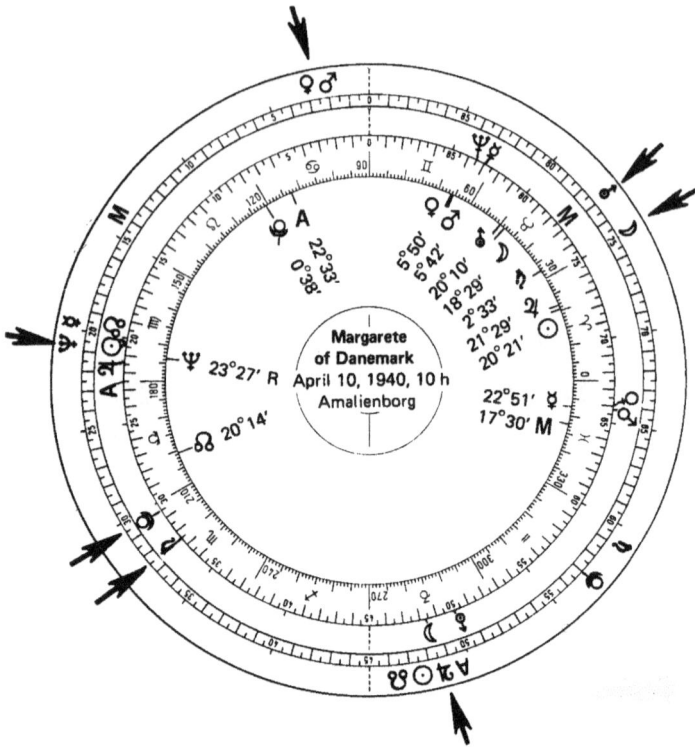

**Figure 43**

ily indicative of a sudden turn (Uranus) in personal (Midheaven) fate (Pluto). Less favorable is solar arc Neptune over the Sun, giving rise to certain disappointments.

In the contact cosmogram (Figure 44), we can see on the right side at (1) his Mars aspected with her Venus and opposite Jupiter and her Sun. This is the configuration that is mainly the foundation of a strong physical attraction. As we will remember from the directions, her Venus and Mars were triggered by solar arc Jupiter. At (2), his Moon and her Midheaven f are harmoniously combined, but her Saturn is located in opposition (4). His Pluto = AS with her Jupiter at (3) can be considered a strong aspect.

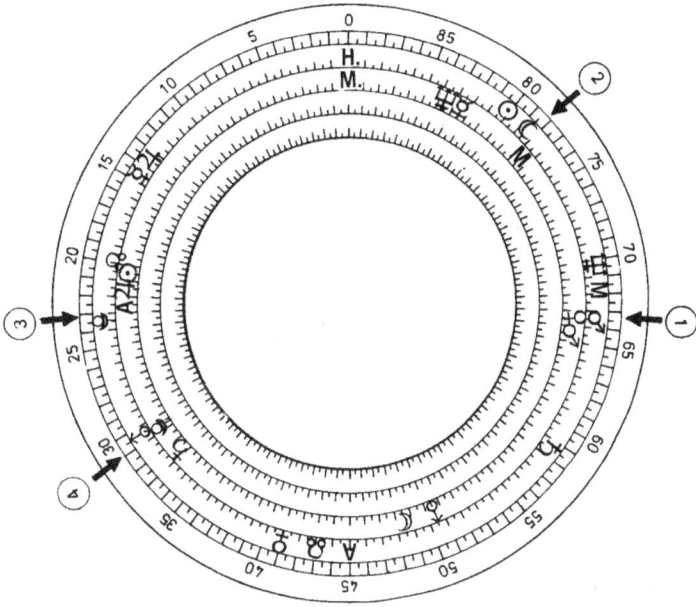

**Figure 44**

In looking at Princess Margarete's annual diagram (Figure 45), we find she chose the right day for the wedding. Jupiter and Pluto aligned, signifying great (Pluto) happiness (Jupiter) in combination with the Midheaven. However, Saturn is also involved, forming a semisquare to Saturn in the radix. Nevertheless, Saturn does not necessarily have to be negative; rather, in this case, it merely underlines the earnestness of the day. Transiting Sun and Venus are aspected with Jupiter and Uranus.

With Prince Hendrik (Figure 46), Sun and Uranus are close together (2/4 in the contract cosmogram), so that his Jupiter = Sun/Uranus also indicates a happy change in life. In his case, Sun

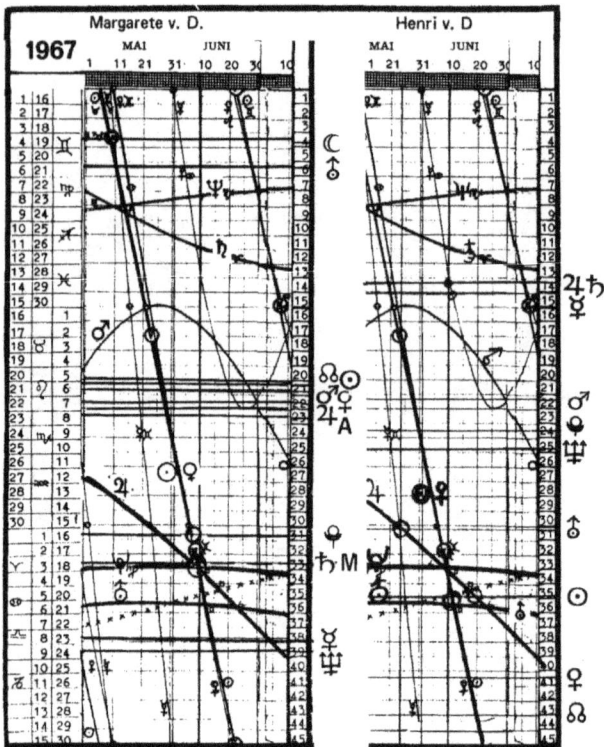

**Figures 45 and 46**

and Venus simultaneously transit the Sun, and Jupiter follows suit in the next few days. The trip through Denmark that the couple took after the wedding was reported to have gone smoothly

With people who are united in love there should be evidence of coincident configurations in the contact cosmogram that indicate common experiences or turns of fate. The prime object is to find such configurations and then to accommodate any joint efforts to the times when these points of contact are activated by favorable constellations.

Hence traditional astrology's practice of allowing an orb of ten degrees in comparing the horoscopes of couples is not correct since the simultaneous resolution of certain configurations takes place in that case not only days but weeks and months apart. Responsible advice must be founded on correspondences as exact to the degree as possible.

# Chapter 14

# Marriage Crisis and Attempted Suicide

We can outline the 1967 annual diagram of Sigrid Bauer, born March 31, 1944, 2:00 p.m., 13E30, 49N00, as follows:

Saturn and Uranus transited the Midheaven in January 1967 and thus indicated unrest and trouble. She wanted to go her own way, but only encountered difficulties with which she could not properly cope. In order to eliminate the necessity of going through all the correspondences of the configurations, turn your attention to the transit combinations in the appendix, which have been numbered for this purpose, Cf. TC 39 and 52.

In March, Saturn transited Mars (TC 31), Jupiter (TC 32), and Neptune (TC 35). All efforts were met with resistance, and there were difficulties in achieving her own aims. Emotional depression and unbalance were the result.

Jupiter, stationary on the position line of Mercury at the same time, allowed for the development of new plans. But there was no release in tension under Uranus over Saturn (TC 46) and Pluto (TC 49). Concurrently, Pluto was involved in an aspect of several months duration with the Node (TC 76). During this time, associations with others were of the greatest significance.

Very favorable Jupiter transits over Venus (TC 17) and Node

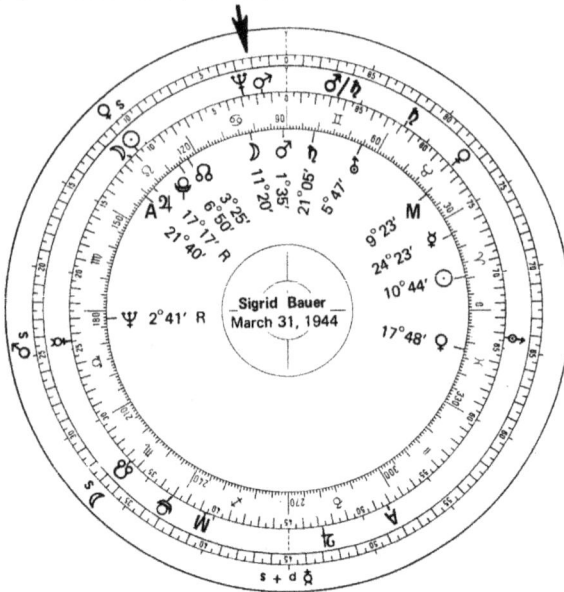

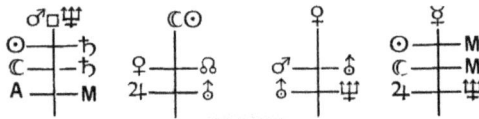

*Figure 47*

(TC 24) developed in June, which can mean happiness in a relationship. However, Saturn over Sun (TC 27) and Moon (TC 28) was in direct contradiction, from which we conclude the possibility of estrangement.

The transits of Uranus over Saturn and Uranus repeated themselves, and Neptune maintained its aspect with the Ascendant for quite a while (TC 64). In September, there was a new clustering of critical aspects of Saturn over Sun and Moon and Uranus over MC (TC 52). Stress can increase. Jupiter over Sun (TC 14) and Moon (TC 15) hardly provides adequate compensation for Pluto over Saturn and Uranus at the end of September and the beginning of

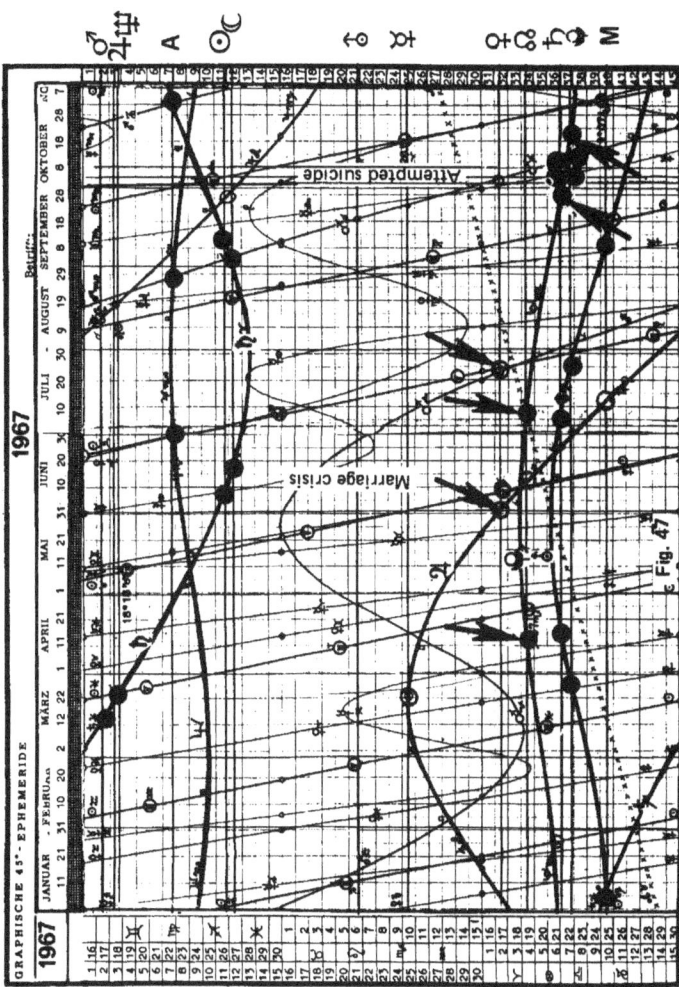

*Figure 48*

October. At this point, Mars over Saturn and Pluto also became involved (TC 7 and 8) and provided the native with a test of nerves.

These considerations coincide fairly precisely with the actual development of the case history. The facts are as follows:

Signd Bauer grew up as one of three children in normal circumstances. She began menstruating at age fourteen and was always irregular. She married because she was expecting. For two years she used contraceptives, but since about July (probably June) she had been having an affair with another man. Her husband found out about it and confronted her; she then admitted to the affair. Her husband wanted a divorce, and an appointment with the lawyer was made for October 2, 1967.

Before they went to the lawyer, she swallowed thirty sleeping tablets and fell asleep in the car. Her husband immediately brought her to the hospital. Treatment began on October 2 at 3:15 p.m. Sixty hours later, in the evening of October 4, she regained consciousness. She stated that she had acted completely on impulse.

The first aspect of notice is Mars with Neptune in the 90° circle, and this at the midpoints Sun/Saturn, Moon/Saturn, Ascendant/Mercury. Even these suffice to indicate emotional crises, especially when the feeling of isolation and loneliness are present. Depression and psychic unbalance could also develop, possibly as the result of disappointment. Progressed Mercury and solar arc Mercury both turn up in this configuration in 1967, indicating absentmindedness and weak nerves.

Sun and Moon are decisive for matters of love and marriage and the relationship between man and woman. Here they are square to one another and in the 90° circle are in conjunction. A happy love relationship should actually develop from Venus/Moon's Node = Jupiter/Uranus. In 1967, this planetary picture was joined by Venus. This means love (Venus) between man and woman (Sun/Moon). But the cosmos does not concern itself with marriage vows. Peculiarly enough, Saturn transited the position line of Sun and Moon twice and, in effect, severed the marriage bonds, with love being sought elsewhere.

Venus, as the planet of love, is located in the radix at the midpoints Mars/ Uranus = Uranus/Neptune. From this results a strong and passionate excitability that is in great need of fulfillment. The cause of the irregular menstruation cycle beginning at age fourteen can also be found in this configuration. In those years, solar arc Uranus square Venus and solar arc Venus square Mars opposition Neptune were in effect. Venus at Uranus/Neptune gave rise to the inclination to dream and idolize, totally ignoring the realities of life. Solar arc Moon conjunct Moon's Node = Venus/Saturn produced the inclination for an adulterous relationship. Solar arc Mars square Mercury led to involvement in conflict, and irresponsibility is intrinsic in Jupiter/Neptune.

We see from these observations that the directions together with the radix already gave an indication of what was subsequently triggered by the configurations in the annual diagram. Cosmobiological consultation would surely have helped the native to find the right path in the face of her troubles.

Chapter 15

# King Constantine and Queen Annemarie

King Constantine and Queen Annemarie became engaged in February 1963. In view of his father's death on March 6, 1964, the crown prince was unable to set an early date for the wedding. The marriage took place September 18, 1964, in Athens. (Unfortunately, we do not have their birth times.)

In the section from the annual diagram, the king's position lines are heavily drawn, and those for the queen are dotted lines. One point of contact is very obvious: the king's Venus and the queen's Mars coincide; in actual fact, they form a square. Without considering the personal points, we only find a few transits for the day of the wedding. The wedding itself was of course only an external and formal affair; the actual union took place a few days later.

Very obvious is that Sun, Mercury, and Venus transited the mutual point of contact around October 8 (Figure 52). There were consequences of this love configuration, which can easily be checked on. October 8 is the 281st day of the year. Adding the usual 273 days of pregnancy to this, we get 55 days. Subtracting one year consisting of 365 days, we get a resulting 190 days. The

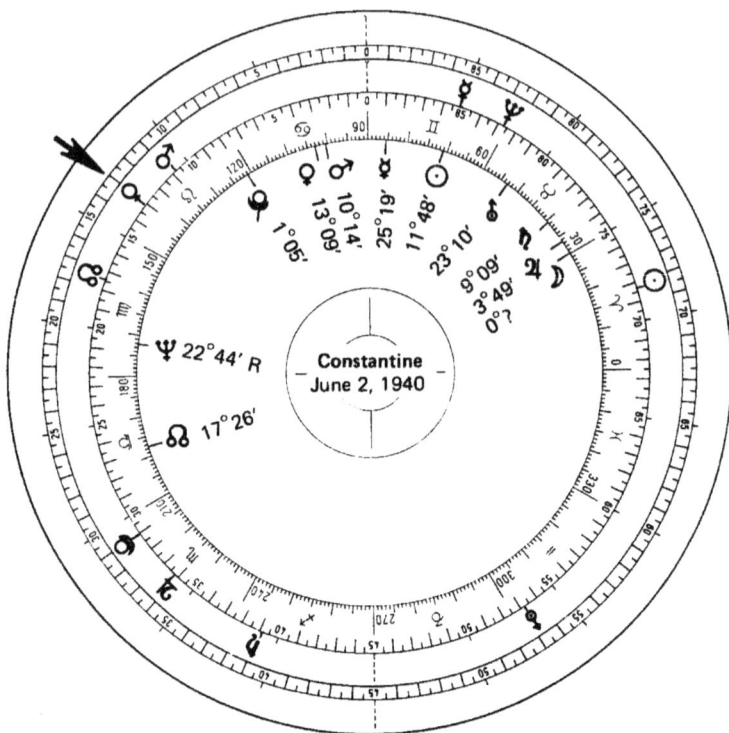

**Figure 49**

190th day of the year is July 9. Princess Alexia, the first child, was born July 10, 1965.

The year 1967 was especially eventful for the royal couple (Figure 53). The coup d'etat carried out by arch-conservative army officers occurred April 21; on May 20, Prince Paul was born; and on December 13, 1967, came the king's counter thrust, which failed, and he was forced to flee the country, unable to return to his throne.

It is typical that at the birth of the prince the Venus-Mars aspect (see (1) in Figure 51) was triggered in the case of both partners by Sun and Mercury. Shortly after the birth, Jupiter transited one

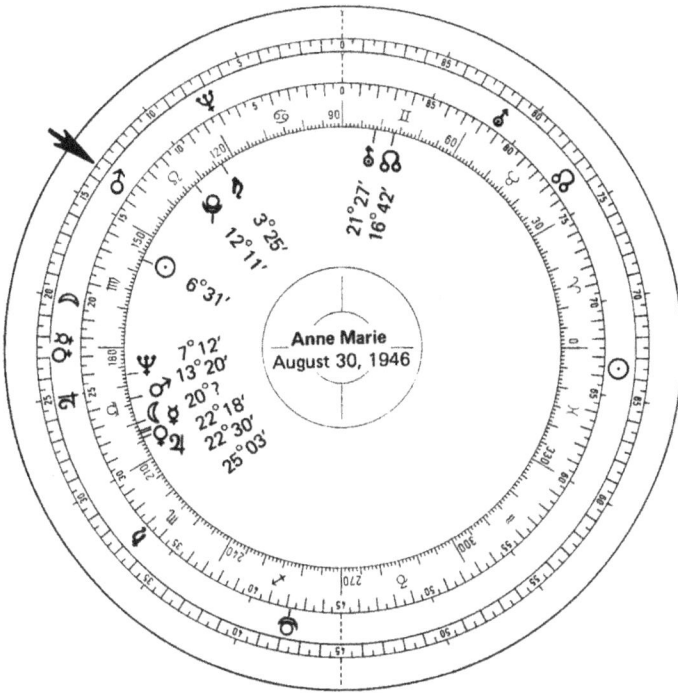

**Figure 50**

other mutual point, i.e., the king's Pluto and the queen's Node. Finally, Pluto approached for the last time the position line of Jupiter. The king was able to stay in power, and the officer's insurrection of April 21 was suppressed, to which end Jupiter over Sun also contributed. Pluto aspected with the queen's Saturn indicates her anxiety about the political situation. With the king, the persistent crisis is expressed in Neptune and Saturn twice transiting Uranus, Saturn over Mars twice, Uranus transiting Neptune and Saturn, and finally, the approach of Neptune to Mars and Pluto to Neptune at the end of the year.

Neptune over Mars designates lack of willpower and ineffec-

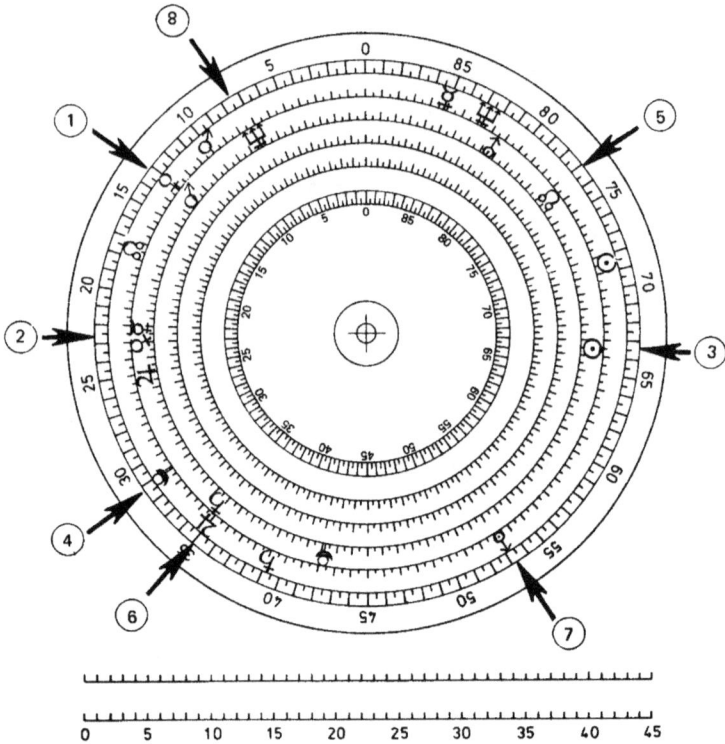

*Figure 51*

tiveness, especially since in the natal chart Mars is to be found at Sun/Saturn. Pluto over Neptune points to unusual problems and serious losses. Please note the many stellar bodies concentrated around Neptune and Saturn (and the queen's Uranus) around December 13. Pluto, Mars, and the Sun are clustered together, so that the king can be thankful that his escape was even successful. In the case of the queen, the apparently stationary Jupiter signals the success of the escape in face of general defeat and the loss of prestige and power.

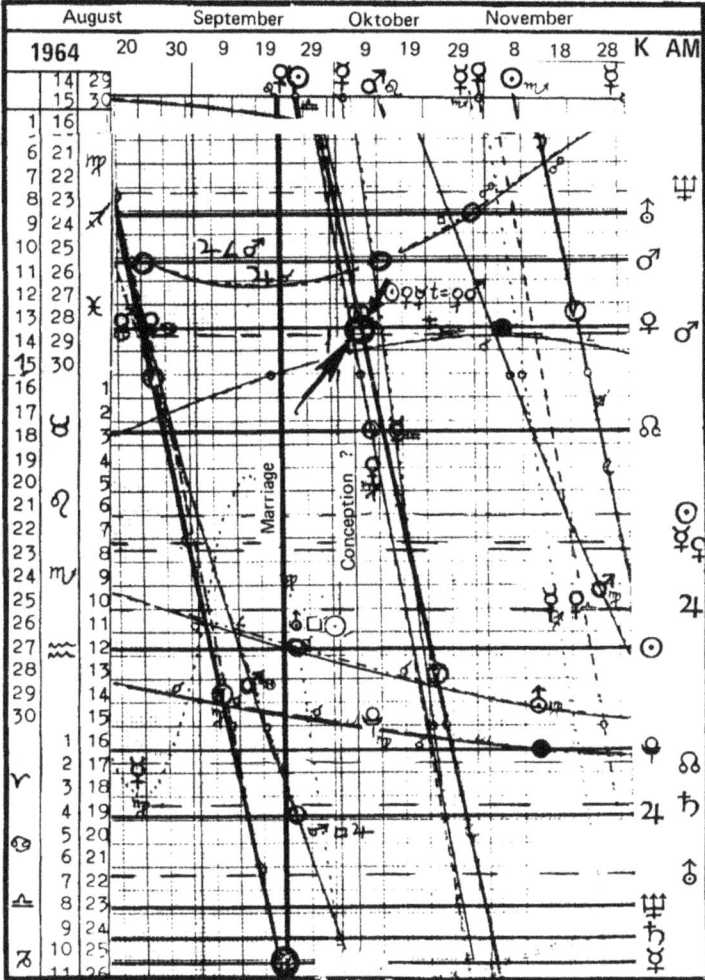

*Figure 52*

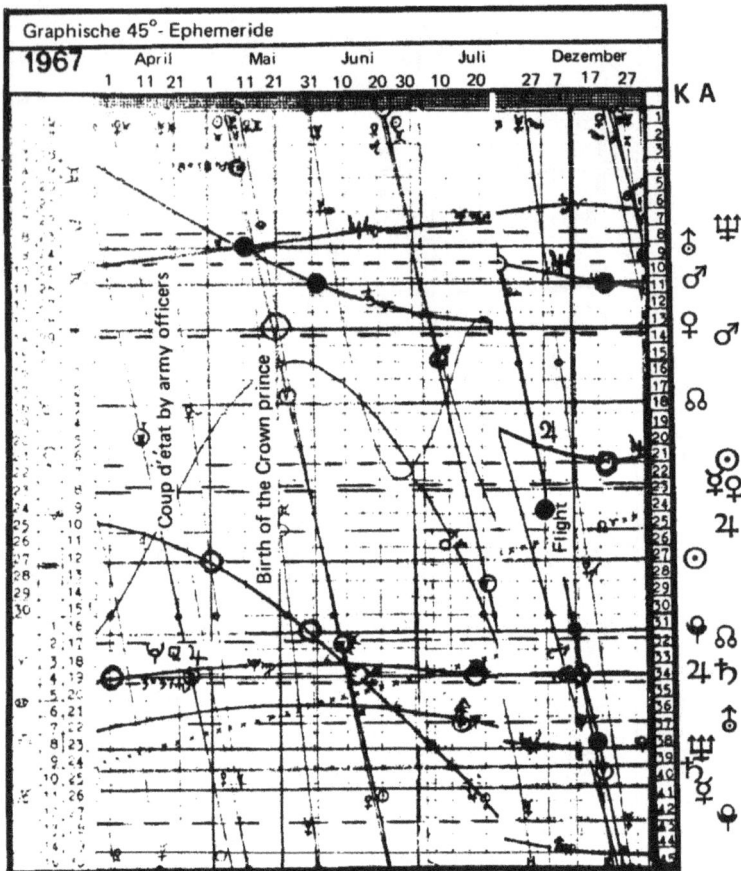

*Figure 53*

## Chapter 16

# Winning the Lottery

A woman born December 9, 1922, 4:45 p.m., 12E29, 50N43, won the grand prize in the lottery on the weekend of April 2, 1960. It was only on the following Tuesday that she found out about it by reading the newspaper. This was the second week she had played this series of numbers. Visits were made to relatives and large presents bought for all. Also, a nice trip was made, and now the couple had the possibility of buying their own home and new furnishings, as well as a larger car, and indulging in a trip to the Mediterranean every year. Seven years later, a new phase became necessary in order to have something left for their old age.

I have pointed out repeatedly that the chances for winning in the lottery are not easy to calculate, and I would like to spare all those readers from disappointment who believe the cosmogram is a sure way of winning. It must be realized that there are a number of factors involved in such prizes:

1. First of all, the possibility of sudden monetary gains has to be present in the natal chart. One such configuration can be found in this case, Uranus = Jupiter/Pluto. This configuration can be interpreted as sudden (Uranus) gain (Jupiter/Pluto).

2. There must be corresponding directions due for the year in question where gain is hoped for. This is also the case here, for in this year solar arc Sun aspected the Ascendant and Uranus. This

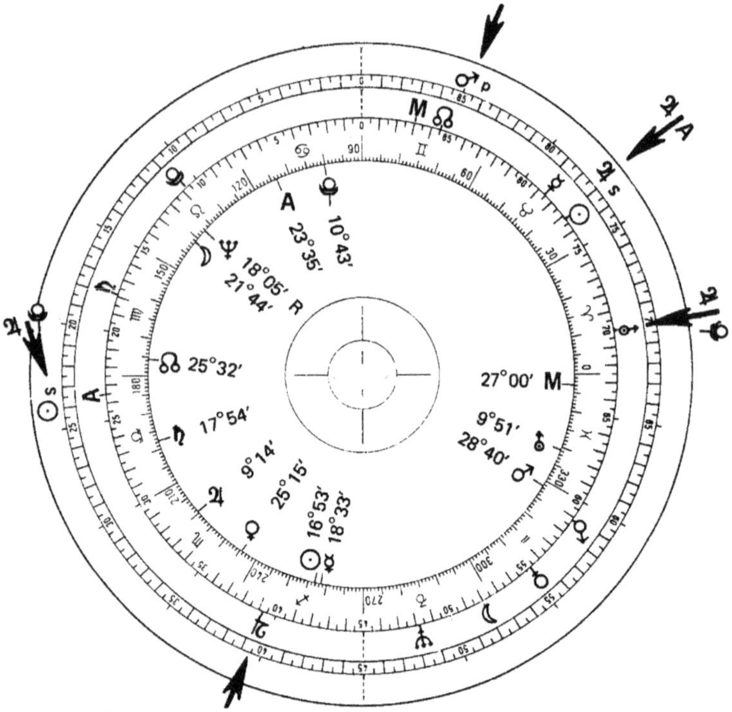

*Figure 54*

indicates an unusual success or gain. In addition there was progressed Mars-135-Jupiter, solar arc Jupiter = Sun (and Mercury) = Jupiter/Ascendant.

3. The potential and the directions should be triggered by transits in the annual diagram. This is also true here. Jupiter aspecting Neptune is indicative of success through speculation or gains without great effort (*The Combination of Stellar Influences* 806). The Sun triggered not only Pluto but Jupiter/Uranus, indicating a happy change in the financial circumstances (*The Combination of Stellar Influences* 795 and 802). Saturn square Saturn had just been overcome.

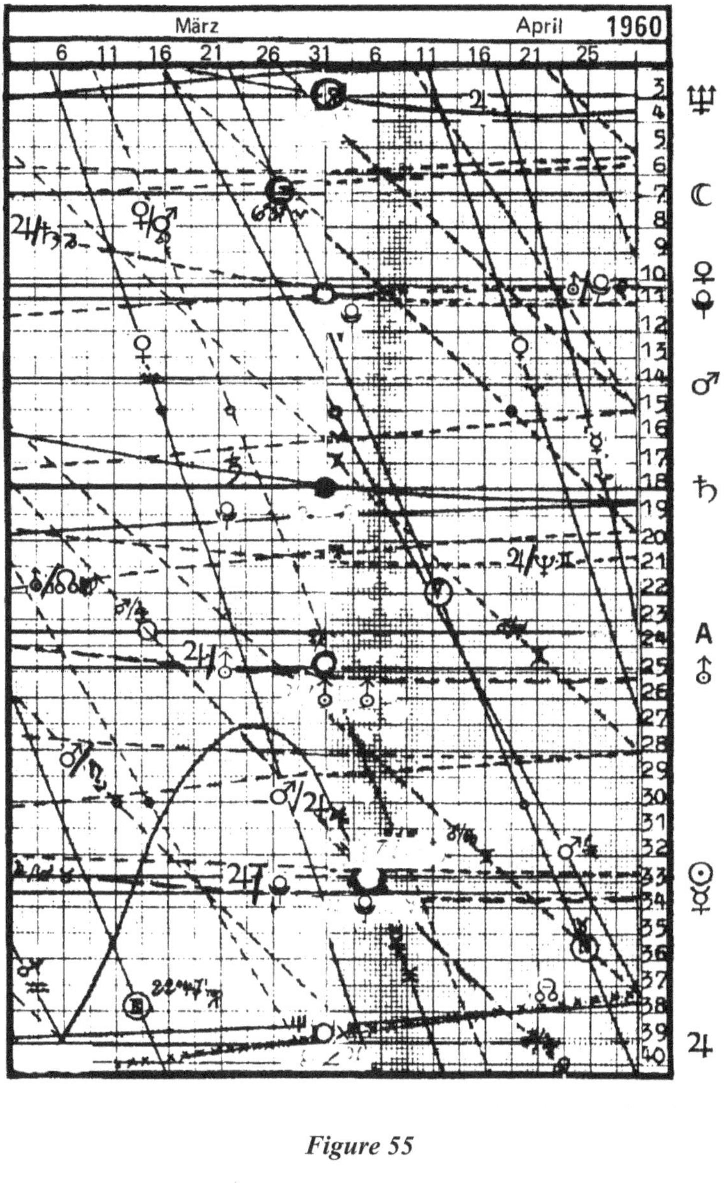

*Figure 55*

The current midpoints were Jupiter/Uranus-90-Uranus, which stimulates the configuration in the cosmogram and the solar directions. The axis of success, Mars/Jupiter, transited the Sun, and Jupiter/Pluto crossed Mercury. Finally, the Node was also a part of a good luck aspect.

This should suffice to show how many factors are indeed at play in a case of some sudden gain.

# Chapter 17
# Troubled Youth

In February 1971, three youths died within a few days of each other. Only the birth dates are available, but the impending crises are readily perceivable.

Richard, born March 13, 1956, was a poor pupil and had to repeat one year of school. In 1971, he was again fearful of receiving bad grades, and on February 11, tied a noose around his neck and hung himself from the door.

In the natal chart, Mercury and Saturn are square. This would most likely mean that the boy was somewhat backward in his development and had a slow grasp of things. Mercury and Saturn are located at the midpoint Mars/Neptune, indicating not only nervous debility but also the misuse of intoxicants, drugs, etc., and instability, feelings of inferiority, and weakness. Due to Neptune at Mars/Jupiter, it must have been difficult for him to achieve his aims, and Pluto at Sun/Neptune points to strain in due to emotional suffering, probably in connection with his failure at school. If these factors had been recognized in time, there would at least have been the possibility of removing him from the school and having him start on vocational studies more suited to his abilities.

In the graphic ephemeris, transiting Neptune had already aspected Saturn and Mercury the foregoing year. We see now Neptune's approach toward this configuration near the time of

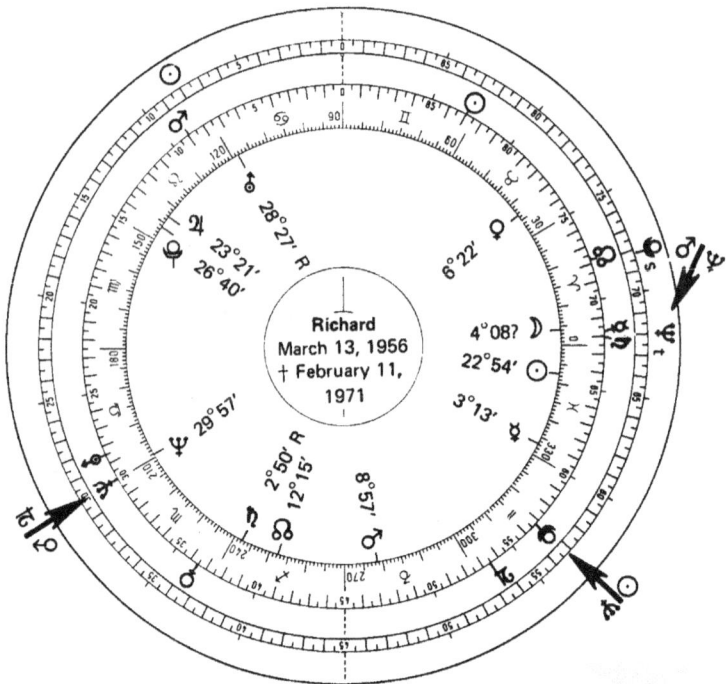

*Figure 56*

death. The boy must have at this time suffered from deep depression to the extent that he no longer knew which way to turn. Since Mercury and Saturn in the natal chart are also located at Mars/Uranus, his act corresponds to the statements given in *The Combination of Stellar Influences* for these configurations (713, 761, 717): placing great demands on one's nerves, premeditated test of strength, violence, energy directed towards separation, grave injury, absolute exhaustion from overtaxing one's energies.

Should the boy have been born during the morning hours, then Saturn would have aspected the Moon for the whole of January, which can correspond to strong fits of depression.

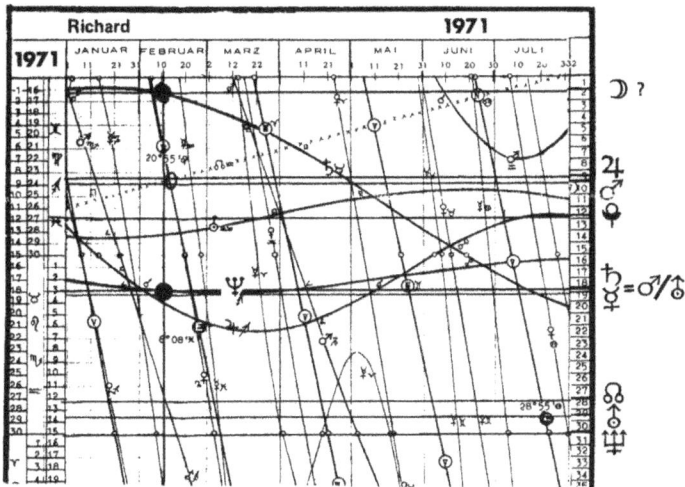

**Figure 57**

Hubert, who was born July 6, 1951, had already demolished three cars, when on February 19, he crashed into a tree and died immediately.

The danger of mishap is evident in the natal chart, where Mars is semisquare Pluto = Saturn/Uranus. Applicable here are *The Combination of Stellar Influences* 871 and 874: occasional misuse of unusual energies, violence, damage due to force majeure.

Whereas in Richard's case Mercury and Saturn were located at Mars/Neptune, Uranus is at this midpoint in this case, as a consequence of which sudden feebleness can be felt, especially when drugs are abused.

We can .see the accident (if it was one) in the graphic ephemeris. Transiting Saturn crossed Mars, which aspected Pluto and Saturn/Uranus, and therefore triggered the configuration mentioned. As is generally known, Saturn = Mars frequently means death. Uranus is aspected with Jupiter and Sun, so it is likely he

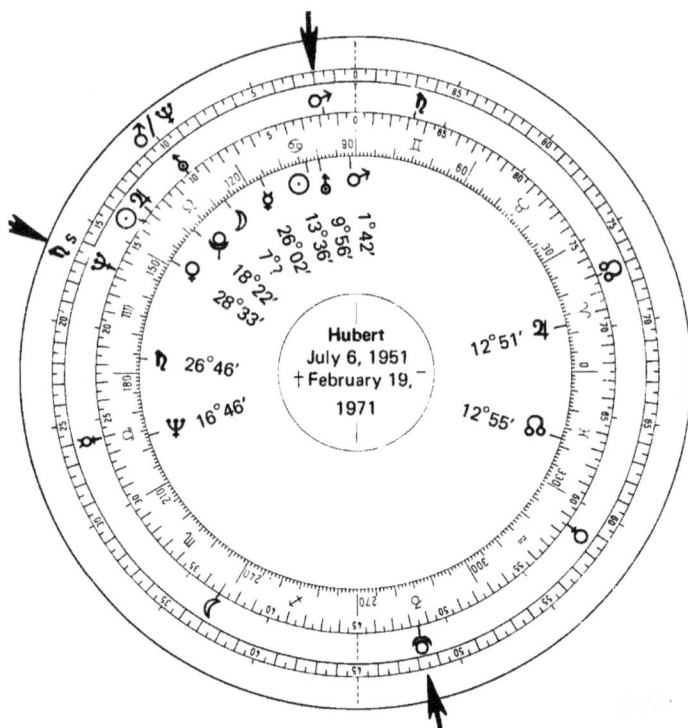

*Figure 58*

had a good time during Carnival. The Sun transits Neptune, in which case we can presume that the youth was under the influence of drugs. Also, Mars was probably transiting the Moon, which corresponds to strong excitement as well as acts carried out unconsciously. The youth was no longer in control of the situation. It is also possible that he was in a depressed mood or was already ill, since the directed Saturn came to a halt at Neptune.

Robert, the son of wealthy parents, born June 20, 1949, was found unclothed February 24 and was probably murdered. His parents heard him in his room with another youth around 3:00 a.m. They did not stop him when he and the other boy left the house.

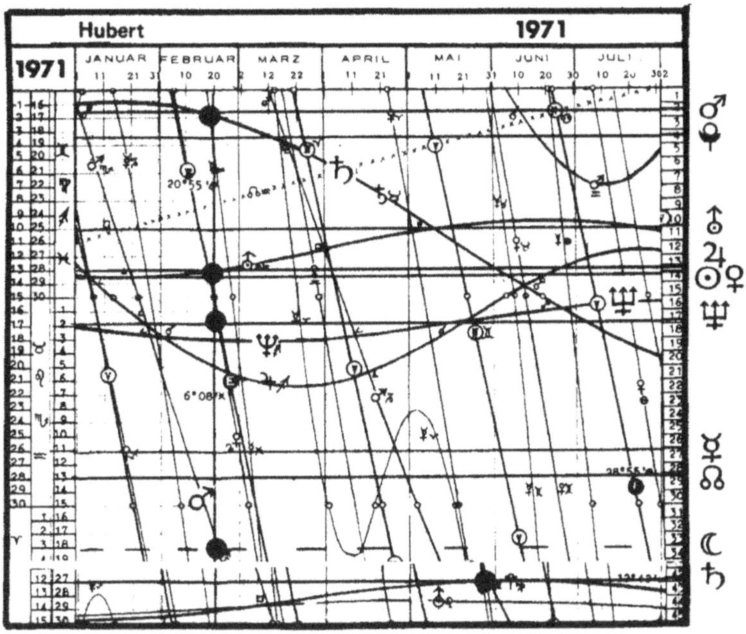

*Figure 59*

Obvious in the natal chart is the configuration of Sun and Uranus, which is located opposite Pluto in the 90° circle. The latter is at the same time to be found at Mars/Moon's Node. These configurations themselves indicate some "tragic experience, severe physical suffering, violent dissolution of a group."

In the 90° circle, Mars is opposite the Moon's Node at Uranus/Pluto. This leads to the conclusion that the native was liable to suffer violence, a mishap or some serious injury at some time or other. Neptune at Mars/Pluto can lead to irreconcilable situations, malice, and harm.

Almost all of the solar arc configurations mentioned above were triggered. Solar arc Mars strikes Sun/Uranus = Pluto and hence signifies injury, mishap, or tragic events.

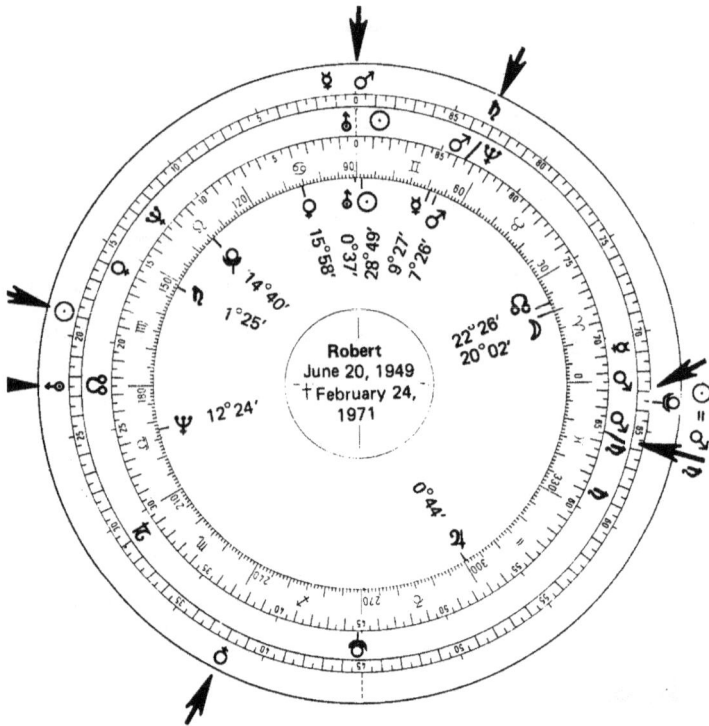

*Figure 60*

The axis of Pluto-Uranus came to a standstill at Mars and Moon's Node and therefore stimulated the potential contained in the natal chart for violence, mishap, and injury. Solar arc Sun at Mars/Saturn indicates danger to life.

The potential and directions as mentioned were indeed triggered by the transits. Transiting Pluto made a station over the complex of Sun, Pluto, and Uranus, and the square to the Sun was exact. Sun and Venus were transiting Saturn. Uranus approached Neptune (= Mars/Pluto), signifying cruelty, violence, and brutality. The native is also said to have used drugs, so he could quite easily have become a victim of others.

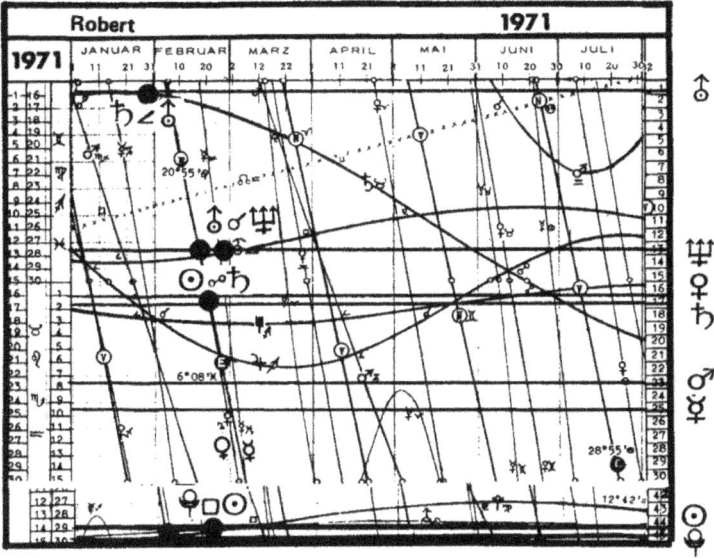

*Figure 61*

Even if we do not calculate the directions, with the help of the graphic ephemerides we can still determine the fact of danger threatening all three youths.

These examples show the merits of occasionally comparing the annual diagrams of the members of the family and making a note of the times when danger is possible. One could rightly say here that caution is the best cure.

## Chapter 18

# The Transit Combinations

The evaluation of annual diagrams using the graphic 45°
ephemerides as a basis requires a different technique. The object
of these diagrams is not to grasp all the details, but rather to obtain
a survey of an entire year and to combine the various indications
given by the configurations.

I would like to avoid the word "interpretation" as far as possible, for we do not try making interpretations in the sense of traditional astrology. Instead, we make use of the tendencies as substantiated repeatedly by similar configurations in numbers of
cases.

The compilation of these transit combinations has been made in
a different form from that used in *Transits* and *The Combination of
Stellar Influences*. It has been found that the individual constellations can by no means be evaluated as purely positive or negative,
or favorable or unfavorable. Rather, one should base one's considerations on a general classification and go on from there to determine in which direction a triggered configuration can have its effect. Take for instance the Uranus transits. These can on occasion
cause a great deal of upset; they can, however, also bring a perfectly good turn in events or bring about a change in life. Or let's
look at the configurations involving Moon's Node. These usually
are applicable to relationships, but without any positive or nega-

tive nuance. An evaluation is only possible here when other configurations are also taken into account. Even if a stay in the hospital is under consideration, this does not necessarily have to be a bad thing because it can contribute greatly to recovery.

The transit combinations of Sun, Moon, Mercury, and Venus have been omitted here, because these bodies generally are active in triggering other configurations. Of significance for an event are the slow-moving planets, although the directions, to which repeated reference has been made, should also not be overlooked.

My guidelines are intended only to serve as a kind of stimulation. Similarly, the native of the cosmogram in question is the best person to evaluate circumstances, once he or she has gained sufficient experience. After all, there are always aspects that are part and parcel of the innermost person and that are not spoken aloud, but which can be essential to the evaluation. For this reason, no calculative analysis, comprehensive though it may be, can replace a face to face talk to ask about the resolution of particular configurations in order to be better able to draw substantiated conclusions and give responsible advice.

The end goal of our research is not only to study the correlations between cosmos and man, but also to make practical application of our knowledge in everyday life.

Uppermost in importance is to redirect our aims from the mere prognostication of events, which could cause suffering for the individual concerned. We should instead aim to draw up guidelines as to behavior and attitudes appropriate to the eventual configurations, and teach individuals how they, with the aid of the cosmic information, can consciously guide their lives, master critical situations, and make use of favorable opportunities.

Those who at the same time work to improve themselves, smooth out faults of character and develop themselves as worthy members of society, and restrain negative urges and show kindness to others will perforce become harmonious individuals and successful persons. They will not easily be affected by adverse influences but can experience true happiness under positive configurations.

The individual shapes his or her own destiny. The cosmic information only makes it easier to find the right path.

The transit combinations have been numbered so that in your analyses you need only refer to the corresponding number instead of having to give a complete description of the combination.

### *TC1*                 *Mars-Sun*
Intensified energy and enterprise promote the power of assertion, the ability to overcome difficulties, and physical performance, making it easier to attain one's goals. The unconscious or unthinking use of this energy can, because of premature action and impulsiveness, result in upset, conflict, incidents, error, or mishap. The use of force, including injuries or surgical operations, is possible in the case of combinations with Uranus or Pluto. An increase in temperature can be expected with illnesses. Those with heart trouble should avoid all excitement.

### *TC2*                 *Mars-Moon*
Energy and feeling are coupled in all activities. A lot can be attained when one does things with verve and interest. One should, however, not get upset and do anything without thinking it over beforehand in order to preclude any disadvantages. Women may not feel well, especially at the New or Full Moon.

### *TC3*                 *Mars-Mercury*
Increased mental keenness is favorable for negotiations and discussions, leads to the realization of plans, and brings success due to eloquence. With some people, depending upon the cosmic state in the natal chart, upset and nervousness will manifest, and with others, this will mean aggression, quarrels, and criticism, and self-control will be required.

## TC 4                                           *Mars-Venus*

A need for love, passion, and impulsiveness may put in an appearance. This configuration is particularly involved in the act of conception, especially when the corresponding points of contact exist between the cosmograms of the two partners. A negative cosmic state can be conducive to extreme passionateness, tactlessness, impudence, and lack of self-control. On occasion, menstruation can be of longer duration and the menstrual flow stronger.

## TC5                                            *Mars-Mars*

Increased energy leads to intensified activity and enterprise, and individual goals can be attained as a result of increased performance. One has to restrain oneself in order not to be ruthless or even violent. There is here a liability for mishap and injury, especially when other transits give indications of such.

## TC6                                          *Mars-Jupiter*

An optimistic attitude, a love of life, the spirit of enterprise, and creativity can lead to favorable decisions, good transactions, and success. One can gain recognition or receive gifts. Many a problem can be solved mor easily, and inhibitions and difficulties can be overcome. Only an arrogant and aggressive attitude can be of disadvantage in combination with corresponding configurations.

## TC7                                           *Mars-Saturn*

Intentions are met with resistance, and only through endurance and indefatigability can certain tasks be achieved. Arrogance, defiance, and an uncooperative attitude can only bring great disadvantages. This configuration may also be involved in bereavement or fateful events. Restraint and self-control are required in all endeavors.

## TC8                                           *Mars-Uranus*

The desire for freedom and independence, obstinacy, and rebellion can lead to conflict. Sudden and successful bursts of energy are possible; however, there is the danger of overexertion, injury, and mishap. Mars and Uranus play a special role in cases of surgical operations. Special tests of nerves or strength may also be demanded. Great caution and reserve are especially required under this configuration. A surgical operation may prove necessary in the case of illness.

### TC9                                                     Mars-Neptune
It is very likely that the will to work and the spirit of enterprise will be inhibited. This may be caused by emotional suffering, disappointment, or even by some kind of poisoning, e.g., through mushrooms, spoiled food, or medication. One should by no means give free rein to discontent, moodiness, and feelings of inferiority. Intoxicants and stimulants should be avoided as much as possible. In some cases this configuration can lead to criminal acts. An improper diet can bring about sickness and nausea.

### TC10                                                        Mars-Pluto
Very high performance in sports is possible under this constellation. There is, however, the danger of mishap and misfortune. Depending on the individual disposition, this transit can evoke ruthlessness and violence, and also the suffering of brutality and violence. Caution and self-control are imperative.

### TC11                                                  Mars-Moon's Node
This configuration relates to people who live or work together in positive as well as negative terms, and thus its influence depends upon the other configurations involved. This transit is also involved in matters of partnership, love, and marriage.

### TC 12                                                  Mars-Ascendant
One attempts to assert oneself in the environment (family, place of work, etc.), to lead or compel others. Others will tend to react to an aggressive attitude with resistance, obstinacy, and general irritation. Conflicts could end in physical violence, but self-restraint is better than provocation.

### TC 13                                                  Mars-Midheaven
The individual strives to realize his or her own thoughts and ideas, developing in the process a great deal of energy and goal consciousness and evidencing the ability to make important decisions.

Precipitous and impulsive actions are to be avoided. Vocational problems can be solved.

### TC14 *Jupiter-Sun*
Several possibilities for success exist at this time. Negotiations can run smoothly, contact with others can be made quickly, or one's emotional or physical state can improve. Arrogance and condescension toward others should be avoided and restraint exercised in eating and drinking, especially of rich foods and alcoholic beverages. Noticeable recovery from an illness may be the case. This and similar configurations can be conducive to a quick recovery after a surgical operation.

### TC15 *Jupiter-Moon*
Enthusiasm for another person or for some special plan is possible, along with an elated mood, and one may also attract the benevolence of others, bringing with it the attainment of recognition or advantages. Contact with loved ones can be especially close and happy. The inclination to generosity and unnecessary expenditure should be kept within bounds. With men, this configuration frequently brings a meeting with a future wife or marriage.

### TC 16 *Jupiter-Mercury*
An especially keen mental and spiritual state should be taken advantage of regarding special plans, vocational goals, matters of organization, agreements, or contracts. Trips can turn out well. This is a good configuration for exams and job applications.

### TC 17 *Jupiter-Venus*
At this time one can appear to be especially attractive and sincere, thus gaining friends. This can also mean especially good contact with the opposite sex that can eventually lead to marriage. It is a propitious time to purchase clothing, jewelry, and objects d'art, and to pursue a hobby. Artists can gain much recognition.

### TC18 *Jupiter-Mars*
With an energetic, positive attitude, it is possible to conduct successful negotiations, to assert oneself in a community or group, to

settle conflicts and differences, to bring about important decisions, and to develop oneself more freely and thus perhaps to commence on a new phase of life. Vocational differences and legal conflicts can occur at times.

### TC 19 *Jupiter-Jupiter*
On days when one can justifiably feel content and much good is coming one's way, it is advisable to give full rein to positive powers, to attain recognition and take advantage of opportunities, and by no means to indulge in pleasure for pleasure's sake. Avoid rich foods and alcohol, which can be harmful to the health.

### TC20 *Jupiter-Saturn*
Perseverance and patience can aid in overcoming any difficulties, and the consciousness of fulfilling one's duties toward oneself can add to self-confidence. Should things not be going according to desire or plan, it is better to take a wait-and-see stance rather than to force things. In order to keep in good health, it is important to pay close attention to diet and not do anything wrong there. Under such configurations, one cannot expect much help from elsewhere.

### TC21 *Jupiter-Uranus*
Inner tensions can be released suddenly, and new perceptions and points of view are possible. The individual strives toward change or is subject to such because of circumstances. A quick grasp of the situation can enable one to meet all demands and take quick advantage of opportunities. Inner unrest or perhaps some revolutionary attitudes should not result in tactlessness or exaggeration, and one should try to settle and not intensify conflicts. This configuration can also mean sudden good fortune or happiness after times of duress.

### TC22 *Jupiter-Neptune*
One indulges in making plans, giving way to all sorts of ideas and exploring one's imagination, but there is danger of getting involved in speculative affairs or of being disappointed. During this time, one should remain clearheaded and not let oneself be misled or tempted, and one should always be realistic in attitude. Those

who do not remain steadfast can become involved in unpleasant conflicts. The statements "undeserved luck" or "money earned without effort" are just as rare as true coincidence.

### TC23 *Jupiter-Pluto*
The strong urge to advance can lead to special recognition or success. The individual's own attitude, however, should be the main contributing factor to taking proper advantage of the chances offered. One's behavior should be such as to preclude any kind of backlash. Should other positive configurations be involved, unusual advancement may be possible.

### TC24 *Jupiter-Moon's Node*
Due to great adaptability, it is possible to come into contact with others more easily, make social or career acquaintances, work well with others, develop good fellowship, or assume a leadership role in a group.

### TC25 *Jupiter-Ascendant*
A good relationship with the environment can develop, and one is better able to maintain contacts in the environment, while being interested in the beautification of the environment. Good relations with others often lead to recognition or success. During this time, existing conflicts or differences can be more easily settled. Success can ensue from public activity.

### TC26 *Jupiter-Midheaven*
A harmonious emotional and spiritual attitude can make relations with others easier, and the individual has new goals and is able to better his or her position. One should be energetic in the proper exploitation of opportunities, especially when Jupiter is moving slowly or quickly over the Midheaven or its aspects.

### TC27 *Saturn-Sun*
It is possible that greater difficulties, family problems and worries, disturbances in health and development, and lack of initiative will arise. In this event it is advisable first to concentrate on the most important matters, to step back and quietly analyze the present sit-

uation and how it can be handled. Contact or cooperation with others should not be the result of compulsion, so as to avoid further alienation or separation. In the case of digestive problems, a light and natural diet is preferable.

### *TC28*            *Saturn-Moon*

Outward events, inner tension and inhibition, and feelings of inferiority can give rise to poor relations and tension. There is no point in indulging in one's moods of depression; rather, one should try to find a way to achieve more self-confidence, come to terms emotionally with the inevitable and unavoidable, and release oneself from inner isolation. There may be some disturbances involving the bodily fluids.

### *TC29*            *Saturn-Mercury*

Do not be precipitous if there are difficult problems; instead, approach them with greater patience and perseverance. Errors are more easily made by those who during this time are unable to concentrate well and are not clear-headed and objective in their thinking. Difficulties with others, alienation, or separation can result from insistence on one's own viewpoint or a biased attitude. A trip can often provide a good solution. The intellectually-minded person should indulge in philosophical considerations.

### *TC30*            *Saturn-Venus*

Temporary sexual inhibition, lack of satisfaction, misunderstandings, and jealousy can lead to disillusionment, disappointment, or alienation in regard to loved ones or friends. Emotional conflict can also be linked to organic disturbances. Special attention should be paid to glandular and kidney activity. With women, abdominal disorders, and with men, trouble with the prostate gland are possible.

### *TC31*            *Saturn-Mars*

Do not despair in the face of unusual difficulties; instead, muster up all the energy possible to master the situation. Intentions will meet with resistance, but this serves as a test of one's own strength and potential. Events may occur that are beyond personal control, where one has no other choice but to adapt oneself to the conditions. There is the possibility of news of someone's death. All use of force should be avoided, and this includes surgery, intensive massage, etc.

### TC32 *Saturn-Jupiter*

When things are not going according to plan, it is necessary to apply a great deal of energy, effort, and patience to achieve one's goals despite the difficulties. The individual should never lose faith in his or her abilities. In a short time the obstacles will be overcome and life will be easier to master. In the case of illness, severe physical exertion and the overtaxing of one's energies are to be avoided; proper care should be taken of the health in order to promote recovery. A change in residence or locality or in relations with others can occur. Digestive trouble can be prevented by eating light foods.

### TC33 *Saturn-Saturn*

There may be signs of one phase of life ending and another beginning. Certain difficulties can arise as a result, but once these have been overcome, life will have become easier again. In such times, it is wise to pause a while, just as the wanderer stops to take a breather after climbing to the hilltop and then steps on at a lighter pace. Turning points are most likely to occur in the seven-year rhythm with the conjunction, square, and opposition.

### TC34 *Saturn-Uranus*

One is impatient, on the one hand, to achieve a particular goal, and on the other comes face to face with difficulties in this connection. In a state of inner tension, the individual has to exert all of his or her energy to overcome the obstacles without upsetting the environment or without getting involved in personal conflicts or disputes. One must, however, resist all uses of force and restrictions in individual development and activity.

### TC35 *Saturn-Neptune*

In the case of emotional suffering, one should take care of the physical condition and health, and when in poor health, one should avoid all emotional stress in order to recover. One will be compelled to concentrate on the self, and effort will have to be made to overcome a particular crisis. Courage and confidence will aid in mastering every situation. A natural diet can alleviate illness.

### TC36                                          *Saturn-Pluto*
Great effort may have to be expended in order to achieve a certain goal, and one may often find oneself dependent upon external difficulties or events that are no fault of one's own. Self-discipline must be exercised and some sacrifices made. All thoughts of being a martyr should be put aside and new problems faced with confidence. Healing exercises and a lot of sleep can add to one's feeling of well-being.

### TC37                                    *Saturn-Moon's Node*
It is not always easy living with others and the need to adapt. It is, however, at times better to show good will and not let alienation or a rupture come about. It is also possible that one's ties with others are based on suffering or difficulties. No meetings should be held in such periods and special arrangements should be made. It may also turn out that a stay in an institution will prove to be necessary, where one will be in close contact with the ill or emotionally upset.

### TC38                                     *Saturn-Ascendant*
When feeling restraint with regard to the environment or when suffering with others, the energy must be found to master the situation and to instill courage in oneself. At times, voluntary self-restraint is better than the possible development of an alienation or rupture.

### TC39                                     *Saturn-Midheaven*
There are times at which one feels restraint in all regards, when difficulties can only be overcome with great effort, and when one sees no possibility of advancement or progress. The only thing to do at such times is to gain experience, exercise self-restraint, do one's duty, and wait for brighter prospects. The day bringing great relief will come, and rapid progress will again be possible. One should not forget the fact that the body, too, needs a respite in order to revitalize.

## TC40                                               *Uranus-Sun*

Inner unrest feeds the urge for change in the career life or alterations in the conditions of life. Upsets involving others are likely. It is also possible for external events or causes to enforce a change. Depending on disposition, an inclination for nervous disorders, heart trouble, or danger through accidents may be at hand. Diversions and recreation should be sought or changes made in one's abode if these are likely to be conducive to relaxation and a soothing atmosphere.

## TC41                                              *Uranus-Moon*

Intense emotional excitability urges the individual to release tension and to realize ideas and plans. The individual also has the strong will to get his or her own way and to fulfill certain ambitions. It will prove necessary to have to keep one's emotions under continuous control. Differences could easily arise in living and working together with others. Ambition can be the wrong trigger for action. Women should be alert for menstrual disorders.

## TC42                                           *Uranus-Mercury*

This is a time of ingenuity, new ideas, and measuring up to any situation. The preference is to do many things at once, but it is necessary to control oneself in order to prevent nervousness or rash actions. There is attraction to diversity, stimulation, and activity, and this inner unrest can best be overcome by pursuing one's many interests.

## TC43                                             *Uranus-Venus*

In connection with relationships with the opposite sex there is a potential intensification, at times impulsive in character, of emotion and feeling. One is more readily able to make contacts, is well-liked, and loves strongly and deeply. For creative persons, exceptional creativity and productivity are possible. Extravagant inclinations should be controlled.

## TC44                                              *Uranus-Mars*

An unusual intensification of energy leads to increased performance. If this energy is misused, there is imminent danger of injury and mishap. Surgery could prove necessary in the case of illness. Obstinacy and the urge for independence and freedom of movement will frequently make their appearance, depending upon existing circumstances and conditions. It is better not to always want your own way.

### TC45 *Uranus-Jupiter*
At this time there could be a sudden release of inner tensions, and one can attain new perceptions and achieve unexpected recognition and success, or there could be changes in one's circumstances. Good opportunities should not be missed, but thoughts should extend beyond only material advantages.

### TC46 *Uranus-Saturn*
On the one hand there is the urge to do something special and different, and on the other there are great inhibitions to be overcome. This results in a state of tension that has to be resolved in some way. One should beware of exciting undue controversy or of rebelling against others or behaving tactlessly. It is easier to handle situations by exercising self-control and through consideration rather than the use of force.

### TC47 *Uranus-Uranus*
One is in all probability at the end of one phase of life and at the beginning of a new period. This transition will take a long time to complete, and one will only become gradually aware of the inner change. There will be unrest and conflict to struggle against until one is again secure in the new circumstances. This is especially true for the time around the 21st, 42nd, 63rd, and 84th years of life.

### TC48 *Uranus-Neptune*
One often suffers because of one's emotional balance, and the thinking is sensitive and unclear with an inability to make decisions. Disappointment can be experienced, and at times there can be detrimental gossip. Relations with others can easily be disturbed if the individual loses control. At times one can also experience an intensification of the unconscious forces, often expressing itself in dreams. However, one should always try to remain objec-

tive and realistic in one's thinking in order not to be misled. Disturbances in the organic rhythms should be quickly attended to.

### TC49 *Uranus-Pluto*

This indicates exceptional efforts because one would like to achieve great aims, carry out innovations, and create new conditions of life. The individual may be confronted with crucial situations and forced to make decisions. External circumstances may also at times play an important part, bringing about new conditions. Reformers and revolutionaries find their way when other positive aspects are involved.

### TC50 *Uranus-Moon's Node*

There could be unrest or incidents in communal life or in work with others that could lead to upset or changes. One should do everything to avoid conflict. In most cases it is advisable to adjust.

### TC51 *Uranus-Ascendant*

One tries to gain more influence over the environment and would like to make certain changes and contact with others, but the individual should also be aware of the possibility of incidents occurring suddenly. This is a time to be in control of oneself and to be able to calm oneself in order to avoid disputes with others. The individual should always keep in mind the possibility of changes or incidents in the environment.

### TC52 *Uranus-Midheaven*

The individual would like to go his or her own independent way, pursue new aims in life, achieve success and advancement, and do new things. Frequently, a change in one's vocation or in one's conditions of life is brought about at this time. However, every venture should be carefully considered beforehand in order to avoid making any mistake. Vocational changes should only be planned when this configuration is followed by very positive aspects.

### TC53 *Neptune-Sun*

Moodiness and impressionability can easily lead to disharmony through or in relation with others, as well as to disappointments, health disorders, or disinclination to work. In this state, one would like to let oneself go and indulge in dreams, and thus can easily lose contactę with reality. Therefore, one should endeavor to free oneself from this negative phase and above all to fulfill one's obligations. Great disadvantages can result from personal indulgence.

## TC54                            Neptune-Moon

At this time one is full of inspiration and premonition and the imagination is especially active, but at the same time there is danger of being deceived, of being unable to differentiate between appearances and reality, and even of being overly influenced by others. The individual tries to empathize with others, but feels misunderstood and dissatisfied. It is necessary to struggle against instability and weakness, and health disorders may also be involved. The circulation should be stimulated, not through pills, which can be harmful at this time, but through exercise, massage, etc.

## TC55                            Neptune-Mercury

With great imagination and many ideas, the individual makes many plans and is very perceptive; however, there is little real energy to realize one's aims right away. The individual must beware of deceiving himself or herself and of making wrong judgements and acting prematurely. Experiences with others are not always the best and no one should be wholly trusted. Precautions should be taken for nervous sensitivity. The actor is well able to adopt a role, the writer is inspired, and the criminally inclined able to deceive and cheat.

## TC56                            Neptune-Venus

Ideals and desires are difficult to realize and fulfill, and the individual longs for love and also tends to idolize, demanding more of the partner than can be fulfilled. There is danger of disappointment and disillusionment. There may also be the inclination for perversity. Beware of intoxicants, nicotine, drugs, etc.

## TC57                            Neptune-Mars

Despite irritability, moodiness, discontent, feelings of inferiority, and poor health, one should try to maintain the usual level of performance and avoid any conscious disruption in contact with others. Errors can easily result from a lack of energy and definite plans. The misuse of intoxicants in an effort to gain energy can be hazardous. Take special care against infections because the body is at this time especially susceptible to poisons of all kinds.

### TC58 *Neptune-Jupiter*

In every endeavor one should try to seek clarity and not be dissuaded from objectivity by others or by some enthusiastic outpourings. Loose and unstable behavior can give rise to gossip and scandal, there can be losses due to false speculation, and the wrong diagnosis can result in improper treatment. Only be convinced by actual facts. At times this configuration is indicative of good fortune such as winning the lottery when the corresponding tendency is contained in the natal chart.

### TC59 *Neptune-Saturn*

The individual gains experience and perception even from unpleasant situations and emotional suffering. In examining himself or herself, there should be no indulgence in discontent or depression; rather, it is the time to be keenly aware of the reality of things and to try to master things through a positive attitude. There is the possibility of illness, and one should therefore take precautionary measures or see a doctor. Those who are always annoyed at something are a source of satisfaction for others, and those who do not let themselves get annoyed will annoy those who begrudge them.

### TC60 *Neptune-Uranus*

The individual should try to avoid bias by broadening the scope of perspective and looking at problems from many sides. It is also wise to with draw oneself from the influence of others, to overcome feelings of insecurity and lack of clarity, and to have a clear and consistent attitude in relationships with others in order not be unduly subject to their influence. One can easily become the object of gossip and rumors. Special caution should be taken with parapsychological experiments and associations with mediums.

## TC61 *Neptune-Neptune*

The individual is broad-minded and receptive to new impressions at this time, and tends to be contemplative and imaginative. However, if a perception of what is real and actual is not maintained, there is danger of misguidance. Pay attention to Neptune's cosmic condition in the natal chart.

## TC62 *Neptune-Pluto*

The individual is burdened with unusual problems and endeavors, and can become subject to peculiar emotional states. But special spiritual perceptions can also be attained. Unconscious forces or even supernatural phenomena can manifest. However, the individual must try always to remain clear-headed. Those who use alcohol and drugs to keep themselves going can easily become addicted. Health disorders with causes difficult to ascertain can occur.

## TC63 *Neptune-Moon's Node*

The individual has difficulty in adjusting to communal life, tends to distrust others, and is easily disappointed by them. Frequently, he or she forms wrong ideas about others or associations. Relationships can be undermined.

## TC64 *Neptune-Ascendant*

The individual can be unclear about relationships with others and his or her environment, and can experience breach of faith or disappointment. It is necessary to draw upon all of his or her energy in order to be assertive and maintain his or her position. It is easy to be misled now, and the individual can disappoint or be disappointed.

## TC65 *Neptune-Midheaven*

When feeling insecure and unsure about things, the individual should limit his or her endeavors and wait until certainty is again present and decisions can be made with assurance. The individual should examine his or her ideals and should not let his or her faith or abilities be undermined by others. Disappointment and loss can be overcome now.

### TC66 *Pluto-Sun*

Depending upon the general circumstances, it is possible to assert oneself, achieve a better position, or realize one's aims. The possible effects extend over a period of up to two years. The individual should guard against fanaticism and overestimating personal abilities. If the natal Sun is poorly positioned, the individual come become a martyr.

### TC67 *Pluto-Moon*

The individual is rich and at times extreme in feeling, energetic and enthusiastic, and has very definite aims to be realized. However, those who exceed the bounds of their capabilities or self-imposed limits, act impulsively, or give too little consideration to others will have to deal with strong opposition and emotional suffering. One should always try to maintain emotional equilibrium and not go from one extreme to the other.

### TC68 *Pluto-Mercury*

It is possible to influence others through speech or writing, to turn every situation to good use, to proceed diplomatically and with cleverness, to attain recognition, and in certain business situations to start an advertising campaign. Overestimation of one's powers can lead to nervous disorders.

### TC69 *Pluto-Venus*

An unusually strong power of attraction and strong feelings of love can result in intense experiences with the partner that occasionally exceed the normal and at the same involve great emotional tension. Lovers should therefore carefully consider whether they can remain together a whole lifetime, and be objective despite the strong physical attraction. Namely, when this configuration has passed, the relationship of the partners can take on an entirely different face. The sexual tie should not be the sole deciding factor.

### TC70 *Pluto-Mars*

There is the possibility of developing unusual power and energy and therefore of increasing one's performance and efficiency, and achieving success on the incentive of one's ambitions. But the misuse of energy can make one brutal and cruel, there could be an accident or surgical procedure. With politicians there is the danger of assassination.

### TC71 *Pluto-Jupiter*

An exceptional striving for power over others or for wealth can be fulfilled to a certain degree, depending upon circumstances. Some considerable vocational successes are in the offing if natal Jupiter is favorably positioned and good directions are due simultaneously.

### TC72 *Pluto-Saturn*

Only with great tenacity and perseverance will it be possible to meet all demands. If one is not careful, one could be cheated of success in work, but the conditions of the times also have to be taken into consideration. This may come into effect if one is in danger of being involved in a natural catastrophe, mass catastrophe, or war. Avoid the use of force. This configuration can be recognized far ahead so that the necessary precautions can be taken. Take special care of health.

### TC73 *Pluto-Uranus*

With great effort and with the expenditure of much energy, one can achieve great aims, carry out innovations, create new conditions of life, and also be compelled to make decisions. Avoid excitement, upset, and potential mishaps. With a positive cosmic condition of Uranus, changes, innovations, and reforms can be successful.

### TC74 *Pluto-Neptune*

The individual is concerned with unusual problems or fantastic ideas, and achieves clarity only with difficulty. It is better to wait to take action until completely sure about things. The individual will on occasion have painful memories of earlier actions or experiences and will have to steel himself or herself to overcome the past. Emotional confusion should not be dampened by intoxicants, etc., which could only lead to addiction.

## TC75                      *Pluto-Pluto*

The individual is at the end of one life phase and the beginning of a new one. The transition takes two years, and at first it means special problems or difficulties until one has come to terms with the new conditions. Generally, only a semisquare is possible, rarely a square. The decisive factor is the cosmic condition in the radix.

## TC76                *Pluto-Moon's Node*

Associations or cooperation with others can be of great significance for the future. If, however, other critical configurations are involved at this time, one can share with others a strange fate or be forced to some mutual destiny (karmic link).

## TC77                *Pluto-Ascendant*

The individual has a great desire to assert himself or herself in the environment, to have an important role in the career, or to make special acquaintances and associations. However, one should be careful not to provoke controversy or opposition if feeling inadequate in a particular situation.

## TC78               *Pluto-Midheaven*

Unusual aims also demand unusual energy and effort. At this time it is possible to take a great step forward, to attain a corresponding position, and to undertake changes in external circumstances that parallel inward changes. It is also possible for outward events to signify a turn of fate. Those who have climbed to the peak should take care that they do not tumble. Close attention should be paid to the cosmic condition of the natal Midheaven.

## TC 79               *Moon's Node-Sun*

The individual can enter into spiritual or physical (love) associations, or relations with the public (newspaper articles, political party, authorities).

## TC 80             *Moon's Node-Moon*

The individual feels spiritually aligned with others. For a man this can mean an association with a woman, and for a woman, association with other women (women's club).

**TC 81**                                    *Moon's Node-Mercury*
The individual exercises the exchange of thoughts with others or feels spiritually aligned or participates in common interest groups.

**TC82**                                         *Moon's Node-Venus*
This configuration is signifies a friendship or a love relationship. One cares about other people.

**TC83**                                          *Moon's Node-Mars*
The individual aligns himself or herself with others through the bonds of fellowship, collaboration or partnership.

**TC84**                                       *Moon's Node-Jupiter*
The individual has good relations with others, is promoted and supported by others, and experiences joint successes.

**TC85**                                        *Moon's Node-Saturn*
The individual feels ill at ease in close contact with others and is disinclined to adjust, preferring isolation instead. The individual can also feel inhibited because of others or be linked with others through emotional suffering (grief). Estrangements should be avoided.

**TC86**                                        *Moon's Node-Uranus*
There will be frequent experiences with others, and the individual is nervous, disquieted, or upset because of others. There is disharmony in communal life, and self-control should be a priority.

**TC87**                                       *Moon's Node-Neptune*
The individual expects too much of others and is thus disappointed. Personal dislike develops and relationships are undermined. Alertness and intellectual and spiritual superiority are helpful in avoiding disappointments.

**TC88**                                          *Moon's Node-Pluto*
The individual can feel somehow bound to the masses, or share in a mass fate or experience a mass event. For a businessperson this can mean association with large concerns. Karmic and fateful links also result.

*TC89*                              *Moon's Node-Moon's Node*
This configuration can be indicative of associations with others, large meetings, and relatives.

*TC90*                              *Moon's Node-Ascendant*
Relationships with others, acquaintances, and cooperation can be involved with this influence.

*TC91*                              *Moon's Node-Midheaven*
Relationships with others are individual in character due to common attitudes, ideals or aims.

# Glossary

AS, or A, or Ascendant: This is the point where the ecliptic cuts the eastern horizon.

Aspect: This means "viewpoint" and denotes the angle at which the individual factors "look at" each other, or their angular relationship.

Contact cosmogram: These charts consist of concentrically connected 90° circles that enable the entering of several cosmograms simultaneously in order to be able to determine favorable or unfavorable contacts and also to establish possible favorable or critical periods (marriage, working partnerships etc.).

Correspondence: This is a connection between the configurations of the heavenly bodies and events occurring on Earth. The word correspondence is used especially where one cannot speak of a planetary influence.

Degree directions: A method of advancing the horoscope where one degree correspond to one year of life. From this movement of two (or more factors), the time of a possible realization of an event may be determined. The directions do not correspond to actual movements in the heavens, as do transits.

Fixed stars: The movement of these apparently stationary stars is so slight that it cannot be detected with the naked eye.

Malefics: This was used to describe planets whose action was said to be detrimental (Mars, Saturn) to differentiate them from the benefics that, according to the old belief in the stars, were favorably disposed towards humanity. For us, these fatalistic conceptions are now defunct. However, it is difficult to find an appropriate substitute. It would be better to speak of negative and positive, although we have to realize that every nature contains positive and negative elements in varying proportions.

MC, or M, or Medium Coeli: This refers to the point of culmination or meridian, which at the moment of birth, or of an event, is at a vertical angle to the birth place.

Midpoints: Angular relationships in which one factor forming an axis is equidistant to two other factors, one on each side, measured on the degree circle. Mathematically, the middle factor is in the half-sum of the positions of the other two factors calculated from 0° Aries.

Naibod arc: This is the mean daily movement of the Sun, which is about 57° to 1°01'.

Orb: The angular relationships of the planets are valid within a certain deviation, or orb, on either side. With the aspects, three to five degrees are allowed, and with the midpoints, one and a half degrees are allowed.

Progression The progression of the heavenly bodies (as directions) is calculated according to the measure of one day after birth corresponding to one year of actual life.

Radix: Meaning root, this refers to the birth cosmogram

Solar Arc: The daily advance of the Sun corresponds to one year of life. The other factors of the birth chart are advanced by this same arc.

www.ingramcontent.com/pod-product-compliance
Lightning Source LLC
Chambersburg PA
CBHW032104080426
42733CB00006B/416